Writing
Above Standard

**Engaging Lessons that Take Standards
To New Heights and Help Kids Become
Skilled, Inspired Writers**

Debbie Lera

■ SCHOLASTIC

New York • Toronto • London • Auckland • Sydney
Mexico City • New Delhi • Hong Kong • Buenos Aires

To My Jada Grace—
Now I'm Found

Credit: Chart on page 86 courtesy of © LitLife.

Cover design: James Sarfati
Cover photograph: ©2005 Image Source
Interior design: LDL Designs
Interior photographs: Debbie Lera, LitLife Archives, and Jupiter Images (p. 166)
Acquiring Editor: Lois Bridges
Production Editor: Erin K. L. Grelak
Copy Editor: Carol Ghiglieri

ISBN-13: 978-0-545-07478-0
ISBN-10: 0-545-07478-9
Copyright © 2009 by Deborah Lera
All rights reserved. Published by Scholastic Inc.
Printed in the U.S.A.
1 2 3 4 5 6 7 8 9 10   40   12 11 10 09 08 09

Contents

Acknowledgments

I've been so fortunate in my life to have been surrounded by exceptional teachers from the day I was born. To all the special souls who so compassionately demonstrated that teaching is best delivered straight from the heart, I write these words for you.

I owe an entire ocean of gratitude to my first teachers, my parents, Jerry and Sue Lera. Your guidance, unconditional love, and support are unrivaled. Dad, your hands nurture life. You manage multimillion dollar projects, cultivate the most scrumptious summer vegetables, and draw my girls' biggest smiles from your warm hugs. Mom, you believe in the dignity of childhood, the importance of empathy, and the power of family. You have both taught me my favorite lessons in life. And to my grandmother, Nella Lera, you have proven that getting older simply means growing more beautiful.

To my rock of a husband, Brian Gowan—you are the best kind of man. You drive a fire engine, read books I don't understand, cook gourmet meals, make children smile, and teach people how to care for others. Your girls cherish you, as do I. I'm so lucky I get to share my life with you. Morgan, my teacher of all preteen things, from texting to a deep compassion for humanity, you are an incredible young lady. Jada, my bundle of baby joy, one smile from you and I'm home.

To my brothers who have made me strong—David, Steven, and Matthew Lera; and to the beautiful ladies you have brought into our family, Esther, Shannon, and Jenna—thank you for the never-ending support. And to Justin and Jacob Lera, the best nephews in the world—you remind me that rolling around on the grass in fits of hysterical laughter is the best thing under the sun.

Thank you dearly, my LitLife family. I am so grateful to you, Pam Allyn, for your insights and wisdom in the world of literacy education. You truly understand children. The trails of your teaching wind through this book. How lucky I feel to have someone so magnetic in my corner. To Jim Allyn, I am so grateful for your business acumen and general sage advice, but even more so for the hilarious East Coast anecdotes that keep me laughing in the car on the streets of New York. ("It's luuuu-dicrous, I tell you!") Thank you both for believing in me. And to the rest of the LitLife gang, my humble heart thanks you for welcoming me into the family and for offering me your years of experience and knowledge.

To my editor, Lois Bridges, you plucked a first-time author out of obscurity and helped me believe I could do it. You are the very best, and I am honored to work with you. To Denise Leograndis, colleague and fellow author, thank you for gifting Lois to me. To the rest of the Scholastic team—Gloria Pipkin, Amy Rowe, Erin K.L. Grelak, Lauren Leon, and Carol Ghiglieri—thank you dearly for your brilliance.

I owe a debt of gratitude to my UCLA teachers—Professor Geoffrey Cowan and all the professors in the Sociology department. You taught me to distinguish myself among the masses with my writing. Thank you, my teachers in the Education department at Santa Clara University. You proved to me that reflective practice is a necessary part of a job that includes affecting the lives of human beings.

To the teachers in Arizona and California, who share their worlds with me and inspire me every day. You are the consummate professionals, the people who bring joy into the lives of children, offering an oasis in a complex world. Your thirst for more, your passion for your work, and sheer talent keep me going.

Finally, to all of the beautiful children who have walked alongside me over the years: you were the reason I couldn't wait to get to school. You were my teachers, too. And to their parents who shared them with me, thank you for the support and gratitude, and for understanding my belief that academic rigor and joy can live peacefully side by side in the same classroom.

Foreword

A miraculous combination of a treatise for success and a practical day-by-day sharing of great lessons for the teaching of writing, this book shows us that we can indeed "have it all"—teaching that is joyful, responsible, effective, and energizing. Debbie's writing is beautiful, heartfelt, and inspiring. Her personal stories, woven throughout the book, reveal a fine teacher-leader who has broken new ground in writing instruction while honoring the goals set forth by state and country. However you use this book, whether as a guide to your everyday teaching or as a book club text across grade level teams, Debbie's wise words will serve as invaluable counsel as you begin a joyful and successful year of writing above the standards with your students.

Many teachers perceive state standards as dry lists that dampen vigorous, active inquiry and learning in the classroom. Debbie shows us how to turn this perception on its head, so that the standards become springboards to dynamic, exciting classrooms that inspire and support the development of young writers. In this wise book, Debbie teaches us that standards can be our north star, our guide, our beacon. She shows us how mandates, structures, and state standards can empower us—rather than victimize or render us helpless—if we create the kind of curriculum and teaching practice that are informed and inspired by both the standards *and* our students. Best of all, Debbie brings dignity to the teaching of writing, so that writing instruction becomes a joyful experience rather than a chore forced upon students (and you).

This wonderful book shares practical solutions for fitting in everything the standards require of us and our students. Through simple and clear demonstration of a unit of study model, Debbie brings us excellent teaching points and lessons with visible outcomes, all without sacrificing the serendipitous pleasures and discoveries of a workshop approach. Through useful planning tools, detailed sample lessons, and meaningful assessments, *Writing Above Standard* will help you craft a year in which your students can flourish as writers like never before.

In this book Debbie shows us how to use the standards to create classroom environments where our children write above and beyond what we ever thought possible. Isn't that our goal, after all—for every student not just to be proficient, but to be learning to his or her fullest and richest potential? Exceeding standards is the true brass ring, and all our writers can reach for it if we create classrooms that are both student-centered and standards-based. This book is a soaring, brave, bold, and beautiful testimony to equity: Every student in your classroom is able to write well beyond what the standards mandate because you are both attentive to the standards and able to provide lessons that take your students to new levels of expertise in their writing.

And now, a note about this author: for the past several years I've had the opportunity to work closely with Debbie. Indeed, she heads the western division of our organization, LitLife. As a professional development organization serving teachers and school leaders, we have a dual responsibility to inspire teachers to love their work and also to make sure our students achieve to their highest possible levels. Debbie has helped us in immeasurable ways to keep our eyes on this dual prize. Debbie is a passionate, kind, thoughtful teacher-leader. Her humanism and expertise together create the kind of teaching voice I would (and do!) follow anywhere. I have seen her in the classroom, gently coaching her students, who love her dearly. I have seen her lead teams of teachers to new heights in their thinking and their practice. I have seen her impact entire school districts with the soundness of her ideas and the practicality of her vision. Her wisdom and her generous spirit are captured in this magnificent book. It is a gift to us all, teachers, administrators, and most of all to all our students who can and will love to write, and best of all, write well.

Pam Allyn
New York, 2008

Introduction

"Let us put our minds together and see what life we can make
for our children."
—Sitting Bull

My husband Brian is a firefighter/paramedic. Each year he takes time out of his busy schedule to come to my classroom for a talk about safety. My first year in Arizona, I had a bright, spunky group of first graders who had loads of personality. For this class, Brian's arrival was so eagerly anticipated that they couldn't sit still. The kids were hilariously keyed up. When Brian finally entered the room with arms full of fire gear, coloring books, and a cantaloupe, all hopes of calm instantly vanished.

That class wouldn't have been the same without Curran, who had more testosterone in his little finger than most men I know. He also had a heart of gold, and he adored me. Curran eyeballed my husband with a furrowed brow and a lot of doubt. I think he was having some difficulty thinking of his beloved teacher having a life outside of school, especially one which (gasp!) included a man other than himself.

Brian worked his magic and won over Curran with his finale—watching what happens to a cantaloupe when it is dropped to the ground with no helmet strapped to it. As Brian was cleaning the cantaloupe "brains" off the carpet, Curran walked up and pointedly stuck his little finger up under my husband's chin. Through gritted teeth and that still-furrowed brow, Curran growled, "You sure picked a good woman to marry!" (True story!)

That was the same year another of my first graders, Kristen, saved our art program. She had heard that it was on the chopping block because of budget cuts and was devastated, so she worked a lemonade stand for an entire Saturday. She marched down to the principal's office Monday morning to deliver the $7.63 she'd earned. A few weeks later, when I announced that our governing board decided to keep the art program, Kristen threw her hands in the air and yelled, "I did it!"

Students like Curran and Kristen remind us that our business is a human one, and also remind us why teaching elementary school is such a blessing and a privilege. There is never a dull moment in teaching, and there are endless opportunities for entertainment.

People, especially children, don't fall neatly into line or fit into boxes (thank goodness). And yet, lately our teaching is defined by standards—checklists of what *all* of our students must be able to do by the end of the school year. To many teachers who absolutely delight in the exceptional individuality of their students, the exclusive nature of these concepts (children versus standards) can be very unsettling.

The idea for this book came from a desire to give you respite from the pressures of your job as an educator in a challenging time. I want to inspire you to illuminate the path that leads toward the kind of writing instruction that feels full and exciting, yet also satisfies the obligations placed upon you as an educator. You need a way to do it all—a way to teach to your writing standards within a flexible and progressive framework that encourages your students not only to meet the standards, but also to rise above those average expectations and ultimately to soar to new heights as writers.

This book will lead you down that path. Your students will begin to adore writing, and you will love teaching it. Writing will become less of a task and more of a creative outlet. Advanced writers will be free to explore new challenges, and your struggling writers will develop confidence in their writing abilities. You will begin to see your classroom as a colorful garden. Your students' writing will awaken, sprout, and blossom all around you, while your writing standards quietly provide nourishment for this glorious show.

It is my sincere hope that in these pages you will find the joy that can and should accompany the teaching of writing in a way that feels natural and rewarding. When children are given the opportunity to create with the written word by an empowered and happy teacher, they produce well beyond the standard expectations placed upon them. Enjoy watching your garden grow!

What Will This Book Do for You?

You care deeply about your students, yet you have limited time and extraordinary pressures. You are looking for tools that will help, and you hope to be entertained along the way. I hope you will find my book useful, thought-provoking and at times hilariously true to the real life we experience in elementary classrooms. To help you best use the information presented in these pages, here are some shortcuts for understanding.

PART ONE

Part One is all about possibilities—for teachers and students alike. Yes, you can help your students meet their writing standards. Yes, you can teach writing in a way that feels joyful and engaging. Yes, you can watch your students blow past the writing standards, achieving levels of skill even you didn't anticipate. In this section, we will begin to examine the infinite possibilities of student writers. We will look closely at sample student writing so that you can come to terms with the infinite writing potential of your students. We will also spend a bit of time considering the writing standards themselves in hopes that you can begin to view them as less of an imposition of limits on your teaching and more as a tool in the planning of your writing curriculum.

PART TWO

Part Two offers pragmatic advice on how to bring above-standard writing into your classroom. In this section, you will look critically at your writing standards. You will discover how to plan a year that balances the four essential skills of writing. You will gain practical ideas about the planning of a strong unit of study. In this section, you will also find several sample units at various grade levels that can be taught in any classroom today. You will find options for relevant assessments that you and your students can use to think deeply about the writing and writing behaviors that are practiced within your units of study. Finally, you will discover very sensible hints about combining content standards into your writing period that will help you meet multiple standards within one unit of study, so that you can make the most of your time.

THE FLOW OF THE DAY

Predictable routines are crucial. Throughout the book, you will note a simple, easy-to-follow structure for your daily writing work that follows the Whole/Small/Whole pattern (see chart on page 11).

FROM THE PLAN BOOK BOXES

Throughout the book, you will notice boxes called "From the Plan Book." These boxes include daily lessons that have been lifted from the plan books of strong writing teachers, and are intended to give you a clear picture of the types of writing lessons you might teach. These lessons are like observation windows into strong writing classrooms. Read, observe, and take them into your own classrooms.

The "From the Plan Book" lessons are intended to exist within a unit of study lasting anywhere from one to six weeks, so the specific lessons addressed would be surrounded by others within the unit. As you read the sample lessons, be sure to orient yourself by noting the type of unit within which the lesson is intended to be taught. As you will discover in Part Two, a well-balanced and comprehensive writing curriculum includes the following types of writing units: writing process units, genre units, strategy units and conventions units. Please refer to chapter 4 for additional explanation of the Complete 4 writing skills.

DAILY LESSONS FOLLOW A PREDICTABLE STRUCTURE	
FOCUSED INSTRUCTION	Students gather for a period of Focused Instruction for 5 to 15 minutes. • Warm up your students with a reference to prior teaching and learning. • Teach one clear point. • Ask students to quickly try your point. • Clarify your teaching point. • Set the stage for Independent Practice.
INDEPENDENT PRACTICE	Students practice independently while you confer with students and/or conduct small instructional groups. • Encourage students to write independently (at their levels). • Have students practice your teaching point as they write. • Meet with individual students, pairs, and/or groups regularly for instruction and assessment. • Look for future teaching points or an example to use in the Wrap Up.
WRAP UP	Students return for a focused, brief discussion that reflects on the day's learning. • Reiterate your teaching point. • Discuss "how it went" during independent practice, noting successes and challenges. • Share examples of student work or learning. • Set plans for the next day and make connections to homework.

The **Lesson Name** identifies the individual lesson (typically one day).

The **Unit Name** identifies the unit of study within which the lesson would occur (typically one to six weeks).

The **Unit Type** identifies one of the Complete 4 components (Process, Genre, Strategy, or Conventions) and anchors our teaching within the unit of study.

FROM THE PLAN BOOK

Lesson Name: *Introducing a Nonfiction Genre Study (3 days)*

Unit Name: *Nonfiction Writing*

Unit Type: *Genre* **Grade Level(s):** *K–5*

Focused Instruction: *Explain to (or remind) your students that nonfiction writing is all around us. Nonfiction writing is true, it is all about one thing, and it tells the reader some information about that thing. Nonfiction writing comes in many different forms, so it is helpful to preselect one form to study that is well suited to your grade level (these may even be specified in your standards). Introduce your collection of anchor texts representing the form of nonfiction you will study. Ask students to explore the collection, carefully noticing what they can about this type of text.*

Independent Practice: *Students work alone or with partners to begin noticing what they can about this unique form of nonfiction writing.*

Wrap Up: *Chart noticings students are making about the mode of nonfiction you are studying.*

Notes: *Some suggested forms of nonfiction per grade level: (K) alphabet books, (1) animal books, (2) biographies, (3) science reports, (4) newspaper articles, (5) Web sites*

Focused Instruction (whole class lesson) details the direct teaching at the beginning of each lesson.

Independent Practice (individual or small group work) links student practice to focused instruction.

Wrap Up suggests a method for bringing the group back together at the end of the lesson.

Notes will further clarify the lesson for you.

The most appropriate **Grade Levels** are suggested for each lesson.

SAMPLE UNITS OF STUDY

In chapters 4 and 5, you will find sample units of study which suggest lessons for entire one- to six-week writing units. The units also follow a clear and easy-to-follow structure.

STORIES AND ENTERTAINMENT

I've also peppered my book with anecdotes from the classroom that are meant to illustrate my points, though honestly they are also meant to make

The **Unit Name** identifies the unit of study and clarifies the purpose of the study.

The **Unit Type** identifies one of the Complete 4 components (Process, Genre, Strategy, or Conventions), which anchors our teaching within the unit of study.

The **Unit Major** identifies the unit's major course of study.

The **Unit Length** suggests the length of time needed for the unit, but is considered flexible.

The **Unit Minor** identifies the unit's minor course of study.

Unit Name: Nonfiction Animal Reports   Unit Length: 4 weeks

Unit Type: Process   (Genre)   Strategy   Convention

Unit Major Report Writing   Unit Minor Organization

DAY	FOCUSED INSTRUCTION (5–10 MINUTES)	INDEPENDENT PRACTICE (35–40 MINUTES)	WRAP UP (10–15 MINUTES)
1 Immersion	Introduce new unit, mark publishing date on the calendar. Give brief description of nonfiction text (true facts, to inform, etc.) Introduce anchor books collected into a bin labeled "nonfiction." Include nonfiction of all types in bin, but take care to include several animal books.	Students explore the books from the class collection, noticing the unique qualities of the various types of nonfiction.	Students share with a partner what they noticed about the various types of nonfiction. Distribute parent note asking students to bring in a sample of nonfiction text from home.
2 Immersion	Have students share pieces of nonfiction text brought in from home. What kind of nonfiction is it (e.g., recipe, directions, newspapers, etc.)? Express awe over how many different types there are.	Students continue to explore nonfiction texts from collection. Students begin to develop an opinion about their favorite kind of nonfiction text.	Students share their feelings about their favorite types of nonfiction. (Place examples of each type on a bulletin board entitled "Kinds of Nonfiction" and label each clearly—"newsletter," "animal books," "people books," etc.)
3 Immersion	Observe new bulletin board with class. "Wow, there sure are a lot of different kinds! I don't know about you, but my favorite by FAR is animal books! If I were writing a nonfiction book, I'd surely want it to be an animal book!" Take a vote: "Which kind of nonfiction would you like to write?" *(Disclaimer: If you don't think this will work, it is perfectly fine to just tell your class you are going to focus on animal books!)*	Once class has decided on animal books, students start to explore only animal books and notice what they can about this specific type of nonfiction text.	Students share what they are noticing. Chart observations.

The lessons in each unit move through four predictable stages (**Immersion, Identification, Guided Practice,** and **Commitment**). The lesson for each day is labeled according to the stage it addresses.

you laugh. I sincerely believe that it is privilege to teach. One of the very best parts of teaching is that we get to laugh every day. So enjoy my stories and perhaps one will tickle you enough to remember that even in this era of impositions on our teaching, the sheer joy of children is the best part of the job.

PART 1

Developing a Framework for Above-Standard Writing

What must it be like to teach without standards or assessments? I imagine this teaching would be a bit like parenting . . . an enormous responsibility, but also joyful and personal. Much like with our sons and daughters, we'd use all our teaching time to really know these little beings inside and out. Our students' passions would guide us. We'd follow their interests as well as our own, and as a result, our lessons would be alive and relevant.

As teachers, we'd have the ability to water the little learning seeds that our students plant along the way. If Max showed an interest in dinosaurs, we'd rush off to the library to check out books. We'd lug back volumes of fiction like *Patrick's Dinosaurs* and nonfiction like *Big Book of Dinosaurs.* We'd read, discuss, pick favorites, make timelines, imagine what it would be like if the T-Rex were alive today. We'd make our classroom into the Cretaceous period and measure the pteranodon with chalk on the playground. Someone would find a chapter in a book that shows how to create imitation fossils, and soon we would be mixing plaster and watching molds harden into replicas of dinosaur teeth and bones. I'd almost feel guilty taking a paycheck, it would be so much fun. (Almost!)

But the real world of teaching is far from "just hanging out" with kids and creating our own curriculum from scratch. In a time unlike any other, teachers today are operating in a world of standards and assessments—requirements that obligate us to predetermined lists of knowledge and skills—the *what* we must teach our students.

We *need* standards for many reasons. For one, they help to regulate the information children receive at each grade level, regardless of the school they attend. Standards ensure parents that their children are learning the "right stuff" when they send them off to school, which can be reassuring when we can't handpick our children's teachers. On a larger scale, standards can help ensure equity of teaching across the vastly different demographics that exist in our country. If all teachers are at the very least meeting their academic standards, then we should be able to guarantee some equity across schools. Standards also guide our preparation, help us plan our year, and help us teach in a way that builds upon previously learned skills. They help us feel as though we are "on the right track" with the information we present to our kids, and ensure that each child receives a varied curriculum that builds upon the previous year. Our standards keep us from playing darts in the dark.

You can probably think of one or two schools at one extreme of the standards' debate or the other. Some seem to have somehow managed to liberate themselves from the state standards. The principal of such a school can wallpaper the entire cafeteria with her daily supply of fresh résumés. What teacher wouldn't want to simply pick and chose teaching points based on her expertise and interests?

Still other schools and districts operate at the other end of the spectrum. Sadly, this is the reality in more and more schools across the country. These districts and schools assume the best way to meet standards is to hyper-focus on them. Standards are the focus of every meeting. They are posted

First grader snuggled into a bean bag with a good book.

Third grader enjoying a book in a comfortable, print-rich environment.

publicly everywhere. These schools may even purchase expensive curricular programs that strictly script teachers and dictate exactly what is taught when. Prepackaged programs such as these leave very little wiggle room for teachers to follow guidelines they themselves craft from their own thorough understanding of the current research coupled with their sensitive assessments of individual students.

Extremes aside, the vast majority of us teach in schools that lie somewhere in the middle of this duality between a standards-free culture and a standards-focused culture. Most of us are under a contractual obligation to ensure that our students meet a list of predetermined goals: *the standards*. And yet, many of us are given the intellectual freedom to choose methodologies that we feel best suit our own teaching personalities and the individual needs of our students.

Tension can result when the teacher's responsibilities and freedoms are hazy or ill-defined. The work of a teacher must be fluid because her students are human beings. Teachers are intelligent and creative people who like to analyze, invent, and create, which is likely why most choose to teach in the first place. More important, teachers are professionals, often with a tremendous amount of education and experience behind them, and as such need enough elbow room to make informed decisions about students and curriculum. These desires may seem in direct conflict to the imposition of standards or an insistence that teachers "teach to the test."

The classroom should be like a happy home: comfortable, relaxed,

First grader trying out her new writing skills.

secure, and supportive. Show me a teacher without a sense of humor about her work, and I'll show you a teacher who is missing out on half of the entertainment! (In what other profession can you grab a cup of coffee and hunker down with a very serious functional essay called, "How to Make a Mud and Worm Sandwich"?) But teachers often feel as though this desirable environment is in direct conflict with the pressures placed by standards and assessments.

First-grade partners engaged in writing talk.

Lesson Name: *Let's Get Comfortable!*

Unit Name: *Launching the Writing Period*

Unit Type: *Process*   **Grade Level(s):** *K–5*

Focused Instruction: *Have students think about when they read or write at home. Explain that most people have a favorite place and position that feels comfortable to them. Some people like to read on the couch, some people lie on their bed to write a letter, some people prefer to curl up on the floor. Tell students that they can do the same in the classroom, because we want our writing time to feel comfortable, just like home. Explain that there will be times that they can work alone in a place and position that feels comfortable to them so that they can do their very best thinking and working.*

Independent Practice: *Students find comfortable spots around the room and test them out during writing time.*

Wrap Up: *Discuss how it went finding comfy spots in which to write. What did students notice? What did they prefer? How did they feel while writing today?*

Notes: *Teachers often ask about what the kids are writing at this time. Since the focus here is on the process of writing and establishing habits, the writing product doesn't matter as much. Part of building self-esteem and stamina for writing in these early weeks includes validating anything they produce. The main goal of this lesson is to get them comfortable and generating text.*

FROM THE PLAN BOOK

Chapter 1

Standards-Based and Joyfully Active—Your Writing Curriculum Can Have It All!

"If I could touch the sky, I would pull a star to hang it in my room."
—Maggie, Age 8

Every year, you thumb through your writing standards in an emotional storm. On one hand, you're thankful for a starting point for your planning process. On the other, you fret. How on earth are you supposed to teach *all* this stuff to *everyone*? How can you truly teach these skills so that your students can perform them independently, even away from the school setting? How can you make sure your kids truly own these skills for the rest of their lives? How do you do all of this in a way that you know is best for them, in a way that preserves the joy of learning and discovering? How can you get your kids to meet all these standards without losing your passion about children and their natural need to discover things on their own?

By their very definition, standards are, well, *average*, but you know your students are capable of more. So how can you approach the standards in a way that enables your students to transcend them, in a way that provides them enough freedom to surpass the average expectations that the standards set?

How you deliver the information is up for interpretation. One way of looking at the writing standards is that they represent a list of predetermined objectives to transmit to your students. In this model, your students are passive recipients of the knowledge. You, the teacher, transmit the information; your students receive it and then regurgitate it on a test. It's as if all students have an empty bucket and the teacher scrambles all day to fill the buckets. The students in this classroom don't do much but wait for things to be added to their buckets.

If this seems remarkably simple, it is. It's too simple. It ignores the most important part of our work: teaching our students how to learn on their own, how to discover, how to go get these interesting bits of information independently—in short, how to fill their own buckets.

Knowing this, you search for exciting new methods in literacy instruction. You read, you attend conferences, you collaborate. In doing so, many of you have stumbled upon the magic of the workshop. You have probably been dazzled by books and professional development about the majesty of the writing workshop approach. Gurus such as Lucy Calkins, Katie Wood Ray, Ralph Fletcher, and Joann Portalupi have spoken to you, rallied you with their captivating endorsements of the writing workshop.

Excited by the idea of the workshop, you also recognize a potential problem. With your standards weighing heavily upon you, you close these wonderful workshop books and think, *"Okay . . . this sounds so terrific . . . but . . . what about my standards? Where do they fit in? Do my standards pull in the opposite direction from a writing workshop? How can I teach in a workshop setting and still give my students a blissful and comprehensive curriculum?"* Tragically, some teachers even reason that an approach such as a writing workshop is *"simply not appropriate for my challenging demographic."*

You are obligated to your standards, yet you want your classroom to encourage active, inquiry-based learning. So how do you reconcile these two seemingly incompatible goals?

Can standards and workshop coexist in a classroom?

Is there hope for active inquiry in today's standards-based teaching environment?

Yes and Yes!

Consider the power of writing instruction that relies upon a standards-based foundation while still addressing the need for active learning through student inquiry. In this approach, you can use the structure provided by your standards but move within that structure in a way that allows you to respond naturally and genuinely to your students.

Consider an example. Second-grade students in California need to know where to put quotation marks. They need to be able to organize a piece of narrative writing so that it flows in chronological order. They need to learn how to write a poem. Second graders need to understand that expository writing has to have some sense of organization and that procedural writing often includes diagrams that help to articulate instructions. They need to be able to write a friendly letter and to persuade an audience.

This list, from the standards, may seem limiting, but it actually provides an opportunity to empower students to behave in a way that encourages construction and ownership of such skills. Teachers can help their students "discover" these skills (and much more). Additionally, teachers can make their students believe that they are extraordinary for making such discoveries, instilling a sense of competence that will carry over into the rest of life.

FROM THE PLAN BOOK

Lesson Name: *What's My Line?*

Unit Name: *Quotation Stations*

Unit Type: *Conventions*   **Grade Level(s):** *2–3*

Focused Instruction: *Print opening quotes and closing quotes on large cards. Say a sentence such as "'My, what big teeth you have,' said the wolf." Assign the following roles to four students: opening quotes, the wolf, closing quotes, and the narrator. Have the students stand up in front of the class in order and perform their roles in the proper order. (The opening quotes player holds up the correct card at the beginning of the line; the wolf says, "My, what big teeth you have"; the closing quotes player holds up the closing quotes third in line, and the narrator says, "said the wolf.")*

Independent Practice: *Students attempt to place dialogue, punctuated correctly, in their own writing pieces.*

Wrap Up: *Use examples of the dialogue sentences students wrote during guided practice to play the "What's My Line?" game again.*

Instead of teaching the standards to your students (simply tossing standards in their buckets), you can help your children unearth them in real writing.

In a recent *Time* magazine article, Nelson Mandela describes his eight lessons of leadership. Each and every one of them is relevant to teaching, but one in particular relates to the theme of this book. Mr. Mandela advises would-be leaders to, "Lead from the back—and let others believe they are in front" (Stengel, 2008, pg. 44). This fits my teaching philosophy nicely. I believe we should lead our students from behind, pushing them toward predetermined destinations while allowing for unexpected stops along the way. We should push from behind because we want our students to believe that *they* lead *us* there—that their decision-making, choices, and actions led to this place of new knowledge.

Although I highly doubt that Mr. Mandela had American elementary education in mind when he suggested these epic bits of advice to would-be leaders, they fit. Teachers are indeed leaders, and as such may as well learn from the preeminent leaders of our time.

The methodology in this book combines the best of two worlds. It blends the idea that you must deliver a predetermined set of skills to your students with the idea that you should teach your students to stay active in the learning process. When you are successful at this, your students will not only discover the standards, they'll mine them out, dust them off, shine them up, and make them theirs for good. But more profoundly, your students will discover and own so much more than just this small list of standards because you are teaching them how to take an active role in discovery and meaning-making, a skill much more bountiful than the standards skills themselves. Your students will far outrun the standards, creating new and exciting and often unexpected understandings of the writing world. Your teaching will feel reciprocal, as you will often find yourself on the receiving end of these discoveries, making your teaching so much more rewarding and enjoyable!

When you plan this way and teach this way, your students will write well above the standards. Follow me, and I will show you how.

Chapter 2

Student Writing— When Above Standard Becomes the Norm

"It is the supreme art of the teacher to awaken joy in creative expression and knowledge."
—Albert Einstein

As teachers, it is not difficult to explain what we do for a living, which is nice when asked, "So what do *you* do?" at a cocktail party or some such context that requires a nicely packaged and concise one-word answer. The conversation usually goes something like this:

"So what do you do?"

"I'm a teacher. First grade."

"Oh, that's cute."

"Cute?"

"You must love all the time off."

"Well, I'm also writing a book."

"Oh! Wow! A novel? No way! What's it about? So I might see it on the best-seller list one day? Wow, you might be famous. Cool! I should get your autograph now so I can say I knew you when. Ha. Ha."

"Um, well, actually I am writing a book for teachers that addresses a particular methodology for teaching writing. I am hoping to . . ."

"Mmmmmmmm . . . hey, do you know where the bathroom is?"

When someone says "I'm a photographer," people are impressed. Photography is associated with an end product that is artful and expressive. What enters the mind is the actual photograph. We think of a black and white winter scene in Yosemite or a beautiful couple smiling in their wedding attire. A photographer is considered an artist, and the value of the work is easily summed up in the product of the work. A photographer's portfolio is all that need be evaluated to assess the quality of his or her work. The product is tangible and explains what the person is up to in his many hours at work.

The writing we collect from our students serves the same function. We can easily assess the quality of a writing program by taking a look at the student writing. (Scary thought, isn't it?) The student writing is the product of a teacher's writing work. Like it or not, our students' writing exposes what and how we do as teachers of writing.

Just like the photographer's portfolio, my student writing is my product. The writing speaks volumes about what I do as an educator, but more important, the end products proclaim to the world that this type of teaching produces above-average writing. This type of teaching produces student writers that soar above standard.

So the writing is where we must start our discussion. The writing proves that students can both *meet* and *transcend* the standards . . . not as an anomaly but as a rule. We need only to read the writing that comes from these types of classrooms to see that all students can write naturally and fluidly. The writing proves that children of all ages can be given the *gift* of writing instead of being burdened with the *task* of writing. Most important, when the samples represent a wide variety of students demographically, the writing proves this works for all students.

Matthew, First-Grade Report Writer

Let's take our first example. In this excerpt from a piece by my first-grade student, Matthew, written during a unit of study on expository writing, the author both meets and clearly exceeds the standards set for first-grade expository writing.

"Hi! I'm Mr. Meerkat. You look like you need some help for research on me. I am the guy for the job! You will learn all you need to know about me. This book will be all about meerkats."

"Yo, dude. I'm a meerkat. I am as big as a ruler. (In box: Why did the Meerkat cross the road? Answer: He didn't!) Yo, dude. My skin is the color of sand. Our tail helps us stand up."

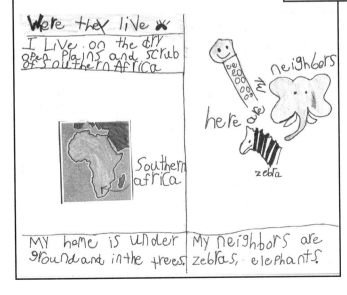

"I live on the dry open plains and scrub of Southern Africa. My home is underground and in the trees. My neighbors are zebras, elephants."

MATTHEW **MEETS** THE FIRST-GRADE WRITING STANDARDS

Matthew meets the required writing standards in his piece. During this unit, I guided my students toward books in which these standards were explicit, and I challenged my students to "notice stuff" about the writing in these professionally published expository books. As they began their discoveries, the children articulated the first-grade standards. They noticed that this type of writing is true and is all about one thing. They noticed that the writing is "clean" (meaning the conventions were in place) and that the authors used interesting words. These new discoveries, from the standards, became teaching points in my focused instruction. The trails of this purposeful teaching are present in Matthew's writing, indicating that he absorbed the new (standards-based) information.

MATTHEW **EXCEEDS** THE FIRST-GRADE WRITING STANDARDS

If I had kept the lessons in this unit limited only to the first-grade writing skills listed in the standards, if I had not honored the other very smart discoveries my students made about this type of writing, Matthew would have met the standards, surely. However, I would have cheated him and all my students out of the opportunity for so much more learning!

My nonfiction unit would have lasted only about a week or two, which is not enough time to do jus-

---

Writing Assessment for "Meerkats" by Matthew, Grade I

☑ Student selects a focus when writing.

☑ Student uses descriptive words when writing.

☑ Student prints legibly and spaces letters, words, and sentences appropriately.

☑ Student writes brief expository descriptions of a real object, person, place, or event using sensory details.

☑ Student prints legibly and spaces letters, words, and sentences appropriately.

☑ Student writes and speaks in complete, coherent sentences.

☑ Student uses a period, exclamation point, or question mark at the end of sentences.

☑ Student correctly capitalizes the first word of a sentence, names of people, and the pronoun "I."

(Adapted From Arizona State Language Arts Standards)

Standards-based assessment checklist.

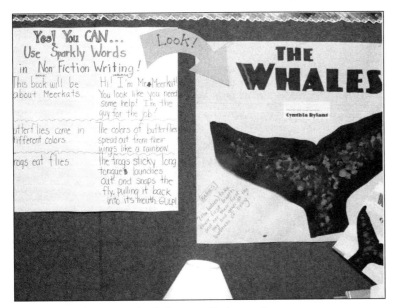

Going beyond the standards in a nonfiction unit.

tice to the complexities of this type of writing, and not nearly enough challenge for Matthew, who was clearly ready to be inspired by this task. Instead, I knew that I wanted my unit of study on expository writing to last at least four weeks so that my students would have the time to sufficiently develop an understanding of this new genre.

I saw that my standards wouldn't give me the amount of material necessary for my students to dive deeply into this genre, but I also knew from experience that the students themselves would surely provide the rest of the teaching points through their discoveries if they were immersed in age-appropriate expository text.

Given the task of noticing everything they could about the nonfiction anchor books I provided, my students noticed much more than the narrow focus of the standards for this grade level. Because they were purposefully exposed to the books I hand-picked for this unit as anchor texts, and because I told my students that they should notice everything they can about this style of text and what makes it unique, Matthew and his classmates discovered many interesting elements of nonfiction writing that went well beyond what they would be expected to learn from the standards.

Here are some elements Matthew and his classmates noticed when immersed in nonfiction writing:

- They discovered that this type of writing was organized into logical sections of information. When reading the Totally Weird series they observed that the information in the books was organized into categories and that each category was clearly labeled. (Student comment: "Hey look—there are chapters and each is about something different.")

- They noticed that there were both real pictures and diagrams in many of these books. In *Desert Song* by Tony Johnston and Ed Young and *Face to Face With Frogs* by Mark Moffett they noticed beautiful illustrations, both drawn and photographed. (Student Comment: "Check this out! This one has illustrations and real pictures.")

- They were very excited to notice that many of the pages in these books had little side boxes with jokes, fun facts, and activities in them. Matthew himself discovered that his favorites were funny and playful. (Matthew's comment: "Yo, dude! Mine has jokes. Listen to this!")

- They were very curious about the labels and captions in these books. In the Eyewitness books and the First Discovery books, they noticed that authors often included words with arrows that pointed to things in the pictures. (Student Comment: "Hmmm . . . these pictures have words all over them. Our story books don't have that, do they? I think they do that to explain what they are talking about in the words.")

- They discovered that these books included a table of contents telling the reader the corresponding page for each section of information. (Student Comment: "There is this table of continents thingy that tells what pages all the sections start on.")

- They commented about the language in these books. In Cynthia Rylant's *The Whales*, Denise Fleming's *Beetle Bop*, Nicola Davies's *One Tiny Turtle*, and Stephanie St. Pierre's *What the Sea Saw*, they noticed that the best books used fancy words. (Student Comment: "I thought these books were boring until I started reading them. There are gems in here!")

- Matthew also picked up on the fact that sometimes the author pretended to be the subject and told the facts using the word "I." (Matthew's Comment: "You mean I can pretend to be the meerkat and tell facts about myself? How cool!")

What tremendous discoveries for a group of first graders! These all seem like very sophisticated discoveries for an average first-grade class, and indeed they are, but they are also very achievable. If I had taught this unit by simply transmitting a list of standards to my class via direct instruction, keeping the students in a passive and receptive role, the learning inside the unit would have been much less colorful. Instead, I allowed my students the time necessary to explore, to notice, and to discover the subtle nuances of

FROM THE PLAN BOOK

Lesson Name: *Interesting Page Design*

Unit Name: *Revising for Clarity and Purpose*

Unit Type: *Strategy* **Grade Level(s):** *3–5*

Focused Instruction: *Tell students that authors of expository text make purposeful decisions about how they design their pages. Authors have a picture in their minds about how they want their pages to look. Professional book companies even have special page designers whose job is to take the author's words and illustrations and arrange them on the pages so they are interesting to the reader. Show several examples of powerful page design in expository texts that include illustrations, labels, and captions.*

Independent Practice: *Students revise expository text to include powerful page design, including illustrations, captions, and labels.*

Wrap Up: *Revisit the reasons for powerful page design. Show examples of successful attempts by students.*

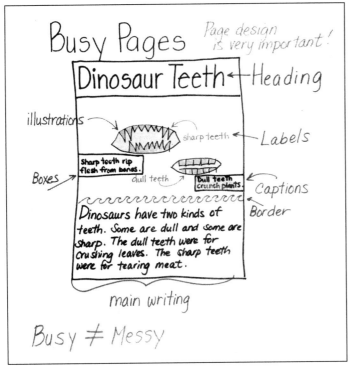

Nonfiction books have unique page design.

nonfiction writing. In their cute little first-grade ways, they articulated the very things that make nonfiction unique. They also noticed some craft strategies that could make their own nonfiction sparkle. These "noticings" provided me with my focused instruction topics for the rest of the unit.

All I had to do next was to simply name the discoveries my students made (labels, captions, table of contents, organization, and point of view) and to challenge the class to try to use these strategies in their own work. And they did! Matthew's piece proves this. It soars above what we might expect from a first-grade student, making his animal report unique and special, and way above standard. Matthew's meerkat information is laid out in logical sections. He includes drawn and real pictures that incorporate labels, captions, fun facts, and joke boxes. He employs tremendous word choice and an alternate point of view. Matthew's silly and creative voice resonates in every sentence. This is very complex material!

Writing Assessment for "Meerkats" by Matthew, Grade I

☑ Student selects a focus when writing.

☑ Student uses descriptive words when writing.

☑ Student prints legibly and spaces letters, words, and sentences appropriately.

☑ Student writes brief expository descriptions of a real object, person, place, or event using sensory details.

☑ Student prints legibly and spaces letters, words, and sentences appropriately.

☑ Student writes and speaks in complete, coherent sentences.

☑ Student uses a period, exclamation point, or question mark at the end of sentences.

☑ Student correctly capitalizes the first word of a sentence, names of people, and the pronoun "I."

☑ Student's voice is loud and clear in this piece of writing.

☑ Student employs sense of humor in his expository writing.

☑ Student writes in multiple genres by including jokes and other activities in his piece.

☑ Student writes in an alternative point of view, the first person, in his expository piece.

☑ Student demonstrates advanced word choice.

☑ Student researched his topic, gaining information for his piece from books and the Internet.

☑ Student incorporates labels and captions.

☑ Student includes sophisticated illustrations and real photographs.

☑ Student includes an "about the author" page.

☑ Student organized his information logically and communicates his intention through the use of section headings.

☑ Student selected his topic based on interest.

(Adapted From Arizona State Language Arts Standards)

Standards-based assessment checklist, including above-standard achievement.

Matthew was able to write well above the first-grade standards in this case, because of the way he was taught. As the foundation for the unit, I pulled teaching points directly from my writing standards. I then supplemented the basics with additional information beyond the expectations of the standards because I decided those pieces of information were important to include. Most important, while Matthew was engaged in this unit of study, I also encouraged him and his classmates to discover and explore this genre freely and independently so that they could develop their own unique understandings of it. I made examples of this type of writing accessible to my whole class, and cheered my students on as they made connections on their own.

Lesson Name: *Introducing a Nonfiction Genre Study (3 days)*

Unit Name: *Nonfiction Writing*

Unit Type: *Genre* **Grade Level(s):** *K–5*

Focused Instruction: *Explain to (or remind) your students that nonfiction writing is all around us. Nonfiction writing is true, it is all about one thing, and it tells the reader some information about that thing. Nonfiction writing comes in many different forms, so it is helpful to preselect one form to study that is well suited to your grade level (these may even be specified in your standards). Introduce your collection of anchor texts representing the form of nonfiction you will study. Ask students to explore the collection, carefully noticing what they can about this type of text.*

Independent Practice: *Students work alone or with partners to begin noticing what they can about this unique form of nonfiction writing.*

Wrap Up: *Chart noticings students are making about the mode of nonfiction you are studying.*

Notes: *Some suggested forms of nonfiction per grade level: (K) alphabet books, (1) animal books, (2) biographies, (3) science reports, (4) newspaper articles, (5) Web sites*

Elizabeth, Third-Grade Poet

Let's consider another example.

This is without a doubt a beautiful piece. It moves the reader. It invokes emotion, and it was written by an eight-year-old girl who is learning English as her second language—not by an eight-year-old prodigy who will be considering physics scholarships at age 12, but by a typical American third grader. This poem isn't even one that she would consider one of her best, either. It is just an example of the type of writing that can flow out of her when she puts confident pencil to paper. She writes every day, and sometimes wonderful things happen.

I found this poem buried in her writing notebook during a writing conference. She didn't even know it was good. She seemed rather surprised when I made a big deal over it. The point is that quality writing becomes natural when children receive strong writing curriculum. It is just routine, something they do. It isn't a struggle. It's just the opposite; it becomes second nature.

ELIZABETH **MEETS** THE THIRD-GRADE WRITING STANDARDS

Interestingly, the only mention of poetry at all in her state's third-grade standards is this: *"Student will write in a variety of expressive forms (e.g., poetry, skit) that may employ: figurative language, rhythm, dialogue, characterization, plot, appropriate format"* (Arizona State Writing Standards, strand 3, concept 1, PO 2). So, clearly Elizabeth meets those, but

Wind

She popped her head
In,
To take a peak.
Then she asked
For tea.
When our silent party,
Was over,
With a flick of her silkskirt,
She disapeered from
Sight,
"Goodby, goodbye wind,"
I said.

Writing Assessment for "Wind"
by Elizabeth, Grade 3

☑ Student writes in a variety of expressive forms (e.g., poetry, skit) that may employ: figurative language, rhythm, dialogue, characterization, plot, appropriate format.

☑ Student uses margins and spacing to enhance the final product.

☑ Student writes legibly.

☑ Student creates a beginning that captures the reader's interest.

☑ Student shows awareness of the audience through word choice and style.

☑ Student conveys a sense of originality, sincerity, liveliness, or humor appropriate to topic and type of writing.

☑ Student uses descriptive words and phrases that energize the writing.

☑ Student applies vocabulary and/or terminology appropriate to the type of writing.

☑ Student uses literal and figurative language in a variety of ways (e.g., imitating, creating new words, rhyming), although may be inconsistent or experimental.

☑ Student punctuates endings of sentences using: periods, question marks, exclamation points.

☑ Student uses quotation marks to punctuate dialogue, although may be inconsistent or experimental.

☑ Student spells high frequency words correctly.

☑ Student uses common spelling patterns/generalizations to spell words correctly.

☑ Student uses the following parts of speech correctly in simple sentences: nouns, action verbs, personal pronouns, adjectives.

Standards-based assessment checklist.

she also meets many of the writing standards listed in other strands, such as the conventions (Arizona state standards are quite heavy in conventions). From this one piece, we can assess that Elizabeth has many of these expected skills in place in her writing.

ELIZABETH **EXCEEDS** THIRD-GRADE STANDARDS IN WRITING

Because the language of the state standards pertaining to poetry in this case is quite vague, Elizabeth easily transcends those requirements. Elizabeth shows an impressive command of poetry beyond her years. It is very apparent that she has enjoyed teaching that focused on the uniqueness of the genre.

In many classrooms today, I still see poetry taught to young children by way of a "poet-

Writing Assessment for "Wind" by Elizabeth, Grade 3

☑ Student writes in a variety of expressive forms (e.g., poetry, skit) that may employ: figurative language, rhythm, dialogue, characterization, plot, appropriate format.

☑ Student uses margins and spacing to enhance the final product.

☑ Student writes legibly.

☑ Student creates a beginning that captures the reader's interest.

☑ Student shows awareness of the audience through word choice and style.

☑ Student conveys a sense of originality, sincerity, liveliness, or humor appropriate to topic and type of writing.

☑ Student uses descriptive words and phrases that energize the writing.

☑ Student applies vocabulary and/or terminology appropriate to the type of writing.

☑ Student uses literal and figurative language in a variety of ways (e.g., imitating, creating new words, rhyming), although may be inconsistent or experimental.

☑ Student punctuates endings of sentences using: periods, question marks, exclamation points.

☑ Student uses quotation marks to punctuate dialogue, although may be inconsistent or experimental.

☑ Student spells high frequency words correctly.

☑ Student uses common spelling patterns/generalizations to spell words correctly.

☑ Student uses the following parts of speech correctly in simple sentences: nouns, action verbs, personal pronouns, adjectives.

☑ Student writes in the poetry genre, demonstrating a complete understanding that poems are characterized by immense beauty of language.

☑ Student employs sophisticated poetry techniques such as personification.

☑ Student uses heightened language to convey a powerful and creative interpretation of her subject.

☑ Student uses imagery to paint a creative picture of the wind for the reader.

☑ Student understands that poems don't have to rhyme.

☑ Student properly uses commas for prepositional phrases and dialogue.

Standards-based assessment checklist, including above-standard achievements.

ry packet" that contains worksheets on the cinquain, acrostic, haiku, blah, blah. This is so limiting, especially when each teacher throughout the child's career uses the same clichéd packet. How many acrostics of his name can a child write by the time he's in high school? Children as early as first grade can be encouraged to "play with words" just like they play with building blocks. They can be persuaded to "just be silly with words" or "really knock them off their seats with words." I tell my students that poetry is the most fun of all the genres (which I believe) because there really are very few rules in poetry. Students can take risks, be creative, and "play pretend" with their words to their hearts' content in poetry. I tell my students that poems are clusters of words that sing and dance off the page.

When children read and discuss poems, the same magic happens that happened in Matthew's class during expository writing. When trained to read with a critical eye, and when given the freedom and support to venture out on their own and think critically about poems, very young children will notice even the most sophisticated poetic devices such as alliteration, onomatopoeia, strong verbs and nouns, imagery, repetition, and similes and metaphors. (For example, noticing alliteration they might say, "All these words start the same.") Then, all you have to do is name the discoveries your class makes. (In this case you'd say, "When many words start the same, that's called alliteration.") And challenge your students to add these techniques to the poems they are writing.

Sarah, Third-Grade Memoirist

Let's consider one final piece. Sarah was one of my first graders years ago. She was in my class the year I announced my engagement and left two weeks early to marry and move from California to Phoenix. I was sick with

Lesson Name: *Personification*

Unit Name: *Poetry*   **Unit Type:** *Genre*   **Grade Level(s):** *1–3*

Focused Instruction: *Begin by telling students to watch while you write a big word at the top of a chart pad. Write "personification." Ask students if they see a smaller word inside that big word. When someone says "person," explain that personification is when an author makes something that isn't alive act like it is alive—just like a person. (Write the definition on the chart.) Give examples such as "the wind whispers in my ear" or "the stars dance in the sky." Explain that the wind and stars aren't people, but in writing and speech they can do "people" things. This paints a really nice brain picture for the reader. Have students think of some examples. Note the examples on the chart.*

Independent Practice: *Students search for examples of personification in poems, then practice writing personification by writing single-lined samples or by adding it to existing poems.*

Wrap Up: *Have students bring their samples of personification to the wrap-up meeting. Students share their new writing with a partner. Ask a few students to share with the whole group.*

Notes: *This is a playful lesson and should be delivered in a lighthearted manner. Have fun with it. Early writers can be more creative poets than older students who become inhibited by peer pressure.*

worry about the impact of my decision that year!

I planned my exit well in advance. I brought my future husband in to meet the class. I talked often about what it means to be a stepmom (and how I hoped NOT to be like the one in Cinderella!) and explained every time I had a chance why I had to move to Arizona instead of Brian moving to California. I introduced the class to their substitute for the last two weeks of school. I kept the mood light and happy, never showing my sadness over leaving my beloved school. (I reserved those emotions for the privacy of my car!)

"And for goodness sakes," I would tell myself, "I was only leaving ten days early! The kids would be fine!" Right?

My last day came and we celebrated. We celebrated my impending marriage and the arrival of Mrs. M, the substitute teacher. There were very few tears, lots of hugs, and many visits from parents past and present. After the whirlwind of that last day, I packed my final box, climbed into my car and bawled. (My mom later reminded me that I cry on the last day of school *every single year*, and that I'd be fine, and so would the kids. Thank goodness for moms who put things into perspective when you need it!)

That summer, I began my new life in Phoenix. I unpacked all my boxes and decorated my new classroom for my first group of Phoenix kids. I pulled out my class photo from the previous year, dusted it off, and placed it right on my teacher desk. I would never forget that last group, and I crossed my fingers in hopes that my first group of Phoenix kids would be as special. (They were!)

Sometime later, I received an envelope in the mail from my old school. This envelope would become one of the most prized possessions of my teaching career. It was sent by a third-grade teacher at my school in California. The envelope contained a piece of writing by Sarah, a student in my last California class—the same class I fretted so much about leaving. A simple note from the teacher accompanied the piece. The note said, "I thought you would appreciate this." She couldn't have known how much I would.

"Unbelievable," I thought. After reading this, I was reminded for the umpteenth time what power and influence we teachers have on the little souls in our classrooms. Sarah meant so much to me, but look at how much I meant to Sarah! I admit, reading this piece reduced me to mush. What a precious gift!

As I remembered Sarah's first-grade writing and compared it to

> # Farewell, Ms. Lera!
>
> Once I was in Ms. Lera's class. Ms. Lera had golden hair, sapphire eyes, and a bright smile. She loved butterflies.
>
> And writing.
>
> We wrote in the morning, we wrote in the evening, we wrote in between. It was in Ms. Lera's class I felt like a writer.
>
> A poetry writer.
>
> Once when I was in Ms. Lera's class, Ms. Lera told us she was moving.
>
> "Class!" Ms. Lera said excitedly, "I am engaged." Before anyone could ask she said, "Engaged is when a boy asks a girl to marry him and if she says yes, they get married. And I said yes! So I'm getting married."
>
> "To who," asked Laurel.
>
> "I'm marrying Mr. Gowan. He has a child. He is a great firefighter and lives in Arizona. And if I am going to marry him I will have to move to Arizona."

2

I raised my hand.
"Why do you have to move to Arizona?" I asked.
"Because his daughter would have to move and that would be very sad, after all she's only a child."
"But were children too," Matthew pointed out.
"Yes," sighed Ms. Lera. "That's true. But she would have to leave everything she ever knew and you would only be leaving your teacher. Well, you wouldn't be leaving your teacher, your teacher would be leaving you."

I thought awhile. What would Mr. Gowan be like? Would he be friendly and good natured like Ms. Lera? Or would he be scary and mean?

Day by day the thought inched away from me, but I still remembered and didn't want her to leave.
What would happen when Ms. Lera left? Even though Ms. Lera had told us that Ms. M. (the substitute) was

nice and I had met her, I hadn't shown her my writing.
What if she didn't like it? What if she hated the topic? What if she ripped it!?!?
I wrote even harder now.
Once when I was in Ms. Lera's class, Mr. Gowan came to visit. He had brown hair and looked just like a firefighter should look, tall, slim and handsome.
"Hello," he said.
And with just that one word, that one word, kids looked ready to faint.
"Well," said Mr. Gowan. He seemed suprised. "Ms. Lera has told me all about you, and you should be ready to learn."
And he started explaining that firefighters are very important and all that stuff.
I decided that Mr. Gowan was friendly and good natured and that

was why Ms. Lera was marry him. But time was running out. Now I only had a few more weeks left to learn.
Once when I was in Ms. Lera's class, Ms. Lera went away.
It happened on a beautiful spring day. One day she was there, the next day she wasn't.
For days on end I walked in expecting to see Ms. Lera's smiling face, but there was Ms. Ms face, also smiling
After a while I got used to her and she liked my writing.
But she just wasn't Ms. Lera.

The year ended peacefully, with all the summer joy. Even though Ms. Lera wasn't there to share the summer joy, in a way she was there, guiding my writing like guiding a butterfly to a flower.

A few weeks after school was out, Laurel and I were looking at what summer activites to chose when a word caught our eye.
"Poetry! It's poetry," said Laurel excitedly. My heart jumped. "I can't believe it, poetry class!" I thought. Let's go show my mom," I said equally excited.

5

But when we showed my mom she said it was pottery.
"But it says poetry, plain as day," we protested.
"No," my mom said. "Poetry is spelled P-O-E-T-R-Y and this says P-O-T-T-R-Y, that spells pottry."

We were heartbroken. We had loved writing. And we still do.

what she was producing in third grade, I also began to think about what this piece said about writing and writing instruction. It came to me at the perfect time. At a time when I was feeling homesick for California, this gem lit my world and invigorated me. It strengthened my conviction that powerful writing instruction is a basic right of all kids, because writing is a basic human skill. I thought, "Yes! This is exactly what can happen with this type of teaching! Yes! The power of strong writing instruction is immense!"

Lesson Name: I'm DONE! (What to do if you think you're done.)

Unit Name: Launching the Writing Workshop

Unit Type: Process   **Grade Level(s):** K–5

Focused Instruction: Greet students with a chart on which you have drawn your best rendition of a student, arms waving high, and yelling in a talk bubble "I'm DONE!!!" As the students watch, draw a big red NOT sign through this picture. Explain that in writing we are never really done. List specific activities students should move on to if, in fact, they find themselves ready to scream out "I'm DONE!" Depending upon the grade level, here are some ideas to suggest: reread your writing, read your piece to a partner, revise your piece, add more to your piece, check the charts on the walls for more ideas, start a new piece, work on illustrations.

Independent Practice: Students practice keeping themselves occupied with acceptable activities for the entire writing period. If they feel the words "I'm DONE" about to bubble up and burst forth audibly, they should check the new list of alternatives.

Wrap Up: Ask if anyone made a great choice about what to do during IP. Have them share their thought processes with the class. Celebrate (like a wild person) those terrific choices.

Notes: Use the book Chester by Melanie Watt for K–2 students. In this book, Chester is never done using his writing pen. He always has something to add to the story or picture. Use the book Love That Dog by Sharon Creech for 3–5 students. The main character, Jack, adds to his dog story throughout the entire book.

Clearly, writing is a skill that Sarah owns and uses to her benefit. She commands this writing skill as she does the ability to sleep when she is tired or eat when she is hungry. For Sarah, writing is a method of self-expression, a way for her to proclaim her innermost thoughts and feelings to the world. She has developed a very sophisticated method of articulating her emotions that seems well in advance of what we might expect of a third grader. For Sarah, already at age eight, writing is a life-skill.

This piece also demonstrates what can happen when all teachers at a school site make a collective and unanimous commitment to writing. Sarah was lucky enough to enjoy writing workshop every single day beginning in kindergarten and continuing through her third-grade class. My class was only one rung on that ladder. Sarah was taught, starting in kindergarten, that writing is "just something we do every day." She was taught that some days would be good writing days and others would not, but that some attempt at writing occurred every day because "that's just what we do here."

Because all of the teachers at Sarah's school taught a daily writing workshop, Sarah came to expect the workshop's structure in every class. Instead of spending the first few weeks in each class learning new systems of writing instruction, she began each year with familiar structures that supported her writing learning. Instead of her teacher defining "focused instruction" (or mini-lesson), for example, Sarah simply needed to hear where the focused-instruction lessons would occur each day in the new classroom and what was expected of her at this time. She already knew the rest, and she had the stamina built over the years to allow her to dive right into the learning.

Give your students the tools they need to be independent writers.

THE "PROBLEM" WITH SARAH

I must admit that I had some difficulty writing the following section, though I confess it was a rather exciting "problem" to have. At first, I figured that I'd follow the same format for Sarah that I did with Matthew's and Elizabeth's pieces, showing you a neat checklist of all the ways Sarah met and exceeded her standards. However, as I wrote, the checklist kept growing and suddenly it was filling several pages of my book. You get the picture. Sarah is such an accomplished writer now because of the strong instruction she received that her excellence is difficult to capture on a finite list. The standards seem irrelevant here, a minor blip on her writing radar screen. In the end, I decided to leave the immense list out, calling your attention to just a few of her brilliant writing choices, and leave the rest of her bountiful and creative writing talents for you to notice and appreciate.

SARAH **MEETS** THE THIRD-GRADE WRITING STANDARDS

At the time this piece was written, Sarah was a third grader in California. Her memoir meets the California writing standards pertaining to this piece with flying colors. It is abundantly clear that the teaching Sarah has received has brought her to a point where the average skills named in the standards are just second nature to her. In a time when many teachers are sick with worry about their children meeting the standards, Sarah is nonchalantly blowing on her fingertips and asking the adults in her life what all the fuss is about.

SARAH **EXCEEDS** THE THIRD-GRADE WRITING STANDARDS

The brilliance of Sarah's piece lies neither in the fact that it meets the standards nor that she does so very naturally. The sheer genius of this example is in the fact that because Sarah is so skilled in the average that the standards become negligible in our discussion of the quality of her writing. She is instead able to rise way above average to experiment with additional writing methods that make her writing superior.

Examples of Sarah's above-average skill in writing are plentiful in this piece. They also reflect Sarah's exposure to quality literature. Sarah employs stylish writing techniques known to professional authors. She is very effective at creating a sense of pacing in her writing. With words such as "I thought a while," and the technique of listing several questions in a row, Sarah slows down the action in her piece. With lines such as "time was running out" and "after a few weeks," Sarah speeds up the pace in her piece. (Sarah's third-grade teacher, Denise Leograndis, taught pacing very skillfully, as she is also the author of a book on the matter called *Fluent Writing*.) Sarah also skillfully uses repetition to lend strength and poetic sound to her piece through the repeating line, "Once when I was in Ms. Lera's class." Additionally, Sarah has mastered the art of expressing internal events by stating repeatedly what she was thinking during this experience. Her reader gets a clear sense of the feelings of the participants in her story all the way through. She does this in a way that is careful and purposeful. These writing skills do not occur by accident. Sarah was expertly guided toward these skills by teachers who know how to plan and deliver powerful and joyful writing instruction.

Are These Examples Typical?

Absolutely! I've seen time and again in classrooms all over the country that above-standard writing is typical in schools that adopt a writing approach that is standards-based—one that allows for time and freedom for active inquiry. The standards base keeps the teaching grounded and calibrated to the teaching around it. The rest helps the students fly beyond. The students in these classrooms are expected to meet and perform what is asked of them, but they also have the permission to explore more than just that finite list of requirements. All students in these classrooms are made both responsible and brave.

The Effects of Strong Student Writing

Focusing on strong student writing has many benefits. We share with our colleagues the infinite possibilities of children and their learning. We prove that students should not be bound by a finite list of standards. We demonstrate that all students (whether typical or atypical) have the absolute basic right to go beyond average expectations, to explore and discover the literary world in a way that feels joyful, individual, and passionate.

Dear Mrs. Lera,

We had to let you know about something extraordinary that happened with Rachel last night. Rachel was telling us about her writing in school and was very excited about something called "oma-pee-a." After a few questions, we figured out she was talking about onomatopoeia. It has been a long time since I was in first grade, but I'm fairly certain that I did not encounter this term until much later! We're thrilled to see her so excited about something in school. Last night we sat and discussed onomatopoeia, and we had a blast thinking of our own examples. Thank you so much for giving this gift to Rachel. What a sense of adventure into the world of literacy she is developing!

Sincerely,

Rachel's Happy Mommy

THE EFFECTS OF ABOVE-STANDARD WRITING ON PARENTS

Parents automatically love whatever their children create at school, so their minds are already primed for the impact of quality writing. But when little Johnny arrives home with a piece of writing that clearly sets him apart from what most would expect of an average writer of that age, most parents will thank you for keeping your expectations for little Johnny close to where theirs are—in the stratosphere. You might hear, "I just *knew* he was capable of this. Thank you for proving it!" (You may also hear, in a shocked tone, "*He* wrote *that?*" in which case, just nod and keep your comments to yourself.)

Rachel's mom saw that teaching "above standard" doesn't equate to pushing unfair or overly ambitious concepts on students. Instead, it means simply that you can, as a creative teacher of writing, help your students meet the basic writing standards while simultaneously activating their creativity, voice, and independent thinking so that there is nothing getting in the way of their natural tendency to take their learning in new and exciting directions.

THE EFFECTS OF ABOVE-STANDARD WRITING ON STUDENTS

The effects of strong student writing on the students themselves are even more remarkable. Often, students marvel at their own creations and at times even find it hard to believe that they were able to create such things. All students

Lesson Name: *Apples to Apples*

Unit Name: *A Look Back at My Journey*

Unit Type: *Process*   **Grade Level(s):** *K–5*

Focused Instruction: *Explain that writing is a journey. All writers travel through experiences that make them better writers over time. If you have one, show a piece of writing you did as a child and discuss how you've changed. Or, ask permission to show one of your students' before and after pieces and discuss. Often, children will be shocked at how far they have come.*

Independent Practice: *Students look at two samples of their own writing, one from the beginning of the year, and one from the end. (For K–2 teachers, this might entail your pulling two samples from student portfolios that you manage. For teachers in grades 3–5, this might mean asking students to identify two pieces from their portfolios, which they manage themselves.) With a partner, students reflect on how they have changed as writers. For younger students, a brief discussion will suffice. For older students, written reflection should be incorporated.*

Wrap Up: *Have a whole-group discussion about the outcomes of the reflection period. How have students changed? Why? Where do they go from here?*

deserve that feeling. It is far more powerful than a feeling that you merely met your requirements. Imagine a student realizing for the first time that what he put on paper is worthwhile, entertaining, or spectacular. Quite literally, the student's head raises a few inches, his shoulders go back, and a satisfied smile takes over his face. In male bird terms, he "goes all puffy." It is priceless, and it is what I hope for every child to experience at least a few times in his life.

THE EFFECTS OF ABOVE-STANDARD WRITING ON TEST SCORES

Good writing is good writing, and our standardized tests are hopefully designed to find out if a child can produce good writing. There is no need to frenetically teach to the test three weeks prior to administering it when your students are strong writers. Strong writers—those writers who have mastered the basic skills of writing, who feel confident, who no longer panic at the sight of a blank sheet of paper, will test well. If the writing experience you are providing in your classroom is designed to meet standards and to encourage the transcending of those standards, your kids will master these writing exams without having to endure days of drilled test preparation. Even better, if your students have experienced a writing program that has followed a carefully designed continuum that broadens over time, adding new writing skill each year, your students will test well. These tests are designed to uncover such sophisticated writing techniques as strong word choice, organization, and conventions. When these skills are purposefully built into an excellent writing curriculum, they become second nature to students, mere habits of mind of all strong writers.

The Proof Is in the . . . Writing

It wasn't easy for me to choose three typical examples of strong student writing. I was passionate about choosing pieces from students who might occupy a chair in any classroom across the country, but I risked having my readers deduce that these pieces were chosen because they are "good." I didn't choose these pieces because they are spectacular (though they are) but because they could have been written by any student sitting in any classroom in America. I truly believe that. These are typical results from classrooms that just happened to include an hour of strong writing instruction every day.

By examining typical examples of student writing from strong writing instruction, we can see instantly that there is nothing average about what this type of teaching can produce. It isn't enough for us to simply strive to meet our writing standards when we have easy access to methodologies that enable us to light the fires, stoke the embers of thought, fan the flames, and then marvel at the creations; because in this way, the fire itself will always burn brighter than we expected. When methodologies exist that make this possible (and especially when they are virtually free), it is time to sit up and take notice.

Chapter 3

Befriending the Writing Standards

"I choose to be inspired by experiences I first judged to be uninspiring."
—Linda Alston

When I was little, Christmas at my house was steeped in tradition. We always bundled up and cut down our tree. We always added a new Santa picture to our book, and chose a personal ornament. We always wore plastic bibs at Grandma and Grandpa Lera's house on Christmas Eve for crab cioppino, and we always drove home with our cheeks pressed against the frosty car windows searching the night sky for a little red light. On Christmas morning, all six of us always sat around the tree in our pajamas and opened our presents one by one. And every year, on December 26, my mom always got up, grabbed a cup of coffee, plunked down on the couch, and declared that was her favorite day of the whole year—her one and only day off.

These traditions had a function in our family. They comforted us and gave us something on which we could depend. We all looked forward to spending our holiday season this way, and our traditions instilled in us a sense of belonging to a larger whole that was important—our family. We thought, "At the very least, we have to do that! It just wouldn't be Christmas without that!" Now as an adult, I find myself thinking these very same thoughts when planning my holidays with my children.

Traditions in Schools

The most joyful teaching I've seen includes traditions that tap into the emotions of children and their teachers. Being part of a community means sharing rituals. Traditions belong in schools in that they bind the members of that community. Teachers play an important role in honoring these rituals. We all have ideas of grade-defining activities, those we wouldn't dream of omitting from our yearlong

The Clifford Effect

Setting up my new Arizona classroom meant hanging 47 yards of fabric in July, when air conditioning is no match for 116-degree heat. It was around this time that my new teammates explained that the first grade always did a Clifford unit at the beginning of the year. So being the naïve outsider that I was at the time, I dared ask, "Why?" After all, I'd never done a Clifford unit in first grade in California! The answer, after gasps of shock and horror, was "Because we just always do it . . . the first-grade Clifford unit is a *tradition* here. People count on it."

Oh.

At this point, the Clifford unit was to begin in just days, so I had to dig in and get up to speed quickly. Clifford was not required by my standards nor by the district curriculum, but not doing the unit meant the possibility of disappointing 20 first graders and their parents, whom I now envisioned showing up on the first day wearing red and asking where Clifford was. Luckily, my teammates were willing to share.

So on a bright sunny day, Emily Elizabeth delivered a fancy package to our classroom. Inside, there was a tiny baby Clifford and a note explaining that she wanted Clifford to spend a few weeks with us. Each night we left food for Clifford and each morning, he was bigger. (This of course required shopping all over my new city for different-sized stuffed Cliffords.)

The kids believed that the Clifford (the absolute "real" one) was visiting our room, but he was also visiting the five other first-grade classrooms at the same time. This seemed to be completely outside the realm of first-grade logic. Recess conversations were hysterical. (I came to realize the first strength of the unit—entertainment while on recess duty.)

First grader in room 23: "Clifford grew!"

First grader in room 22: "I know! I saw!"

First grader in room 21: "He chewed up our pencil box!"

First grader in room 24: "Whoa! He chewed a cup in our room."

First grader in room 25: "I guess he was hungry!"

plan, either because of our own emotional attachment to the work or because of a long-standing tradition entrenched in that community. We think, "At the very least, we have to do that! It just wouldn't be second grade without that!" These are the things that make a grade level unique. The dinosaur unit in second grade in which little explorers dig up fossils—we *have* to do that! The wax museum in fifth grade in which students transform themselves into historical figures and memorize speeches—we *have* to do that! The bug assembly in second grade—we *have* to do that!

First grader in room 23: "He told our teacher pizza is his favorite food."

First grader in room 22: "Yeah. He told our teacher hamburgers are his favorite."

First grader in room 21: "He's like three feet now!"

First grader in room 25: "Clifford is soooooooo cooooooool! I loooove him."

First grader in room 24: "I LOVE first grade!"

All: "Me too! Me too! Me too! Me three!"

Never one time did I hear anyone stop and think aloud, "Hey, wait a minute . . . if he's in our room, then how did he . . . ? How is he . . . ? How . . .?" (which is precisely why the Clifford unit happens in first grade, not third grade!)

The second week, to the astonishment of all involved, Clifford ran away. He left a note explaining that he felt cooped up in our classroom (having grown so big) and went for an adventure. The kids were very concerned, and we set out to find him. Our class began to receive letters from older siblings, teachers, coaches, librarians, and administrators regarding sightings of our lost Clifford. Our missing Clifford was the lead story on the morning announcements.

Each day we visited another location in the school, searching for Clifford. My first graders learned where the library was, the office, the cafeteria, the nurse . . . because we had heard that Clifford had been spotted in those places. My students wrote, read, thought, and talked (oh, how they talked) about Clifford. They were very engaged . . .
as was the rest of the school community.

I watched this all unfold with amazement. Magic was happening! This tradition had a very important place in this community. Though they may not always follow specific standards, there is absolutely a time and place for joyful learning around the traditions that help to define the age, the grade level, the school, the community. Hearing screams of "HE GROWED!" every morning that first week, and watching 40 little eyebrows hike to the hairline when Clifford was found in the principal's office at the end of the week, convinced me of the ultimate value of the Clifford unit. It was tradition, and it was just plain wonderful fun.

Traditions Versus Standards in Schools

There is an important place for tradition in schools. Students come to count on tradition. They hear about their older siblings' experiences and look forward to them as well. Grade-level traditions add to the valuable experiences of that year. Traditions that are associated with the school site help to unite the community and to offer members a sense of belonging and common experience.

Though our standards are requirements, traditions may be freely elected activities educators incorporate. This doesn't make them any less important. They may or may not help us meet our standards, but they belong in the curriculum. The best possible scenario, of course, is when a long-standing tradition does indeed meet academic standards. This may not always be possible, but in the most magical of classrooms, both traditions and standards dance gracefully together.

As you think about your own curriculum, you should be articulate in the ways in which your traditions relate to your academic standards. Traditions are those time-tested, anticipated activities you engage in each year, while the standards are what our students must achieve by the end of the year.

TRADITIONS	ACADEMIC STANDARDS
Watching chicks hatch from eggs in kindergarten	"Students will be exposed to various life cycles."
Family-tree project in first grade	"Students will explore the reasons people come to America."
Wax museum in fifth grade	"Students will explore famous Americans and their impact on American History."
Zoo field trip in third grade	"Students will observe animals in their habitats."

Lesson Name: *Friendship Fruit Salad—Final Celebration for Functional Writing Unit*

Unit Name: *Functional Writing—Recipes (10 days)*

Unit Type: *Genre*   **Grade Level(s):** *1–3*

Read Enemy Pie by Derek Munson. As a class, study the structure of traditional recipes by exploring recipe books or recipes from other sources like magazines or the Internet. (The elements of a traditional recipe may include: materials, ingredients, things to prepare in advance, and directions.) Together as a class, write the rather untraditional recipe for Enemy Pie. (Materials needed: one enemy, one backyard in which to play with your enemy, etc.) Have students write their own recipes. Recipes can either be very traditional (a recipe for a peanut butter and jelly sandwich) or very creative (a recipe for friendship). Celebrate the end of this unit with a "Friendship Fruit Salad" in which all students bring in a fruit to add to a giant fruit bowl. Eat the Friendship Fruit Salad and discuss whether Enemy Pie is really "friendship" pie.

Notes: *One of the most common threads running through school traditions is friendship. This lesson presents an excellent opportunity to marry a tradition you may already have at your school with a required writing genre such as functional writing.*

Traditions can support standards, and in the strongest of cases probably do, but don't put too much pressure on yourself in this area. If there is a tradition that you feel is crucial to your grade level (because "it just wouldn't be right without it!") then by all means, include it. What could be more valuable than creating an excitement and outright joy about being in the classroom? Sometimes, the behavior these traditions encourage is that of rushing eagerly to school each morning. What is more valuable than that?

Problems With Standards—
The Four Fatal P's

Standards can be a rather lackluster alternative to the creative traditions designed in the name of sheer fun. Yet for most educators these days, academic standards are not merely suggestions. These formal impositions on your teaching require you to teach very specific things about which you may or may not feel personally moved or motivated.

The standards have a lot of problems associated with them. The push toward academic standards in public education has been in the news quite a bit lately, and the stories usually are not positive. Let's take a minute to clearly understand the current climate associated with academic standards by looking at four specific difficulties associated with them.

POLITICS

Unfortunately, the biggest confusion about standards has been caused by the recent governmental push to equate standards with standardized tests, likely caused by the No Child Left Behind Act. Because of the current political climate, there is a very common misunderstanding within our profession that an educator who supports the use of standards probably also supports standardized testing. Douglas B. Reeves says, "[F]or many teachers, parents, and students, standards have become inextricably linked to standardized tests. If they dislike the latter, they blame the former" (2002, p. xvi).

For the sake of this discussion, let's peel apart these two subjects and take back the potentially positive application of standards from the testing gurus, who have harmed their original intentions. Leaders cannot eliminate opposition to standards, but they can change the focus of the discussion. If the case for standards rests on a foundation of a legal mandate, then the leader mutters with resignation, "It's the law, so like it or not, we have to do it." If, however, the case for standards rests on a foundation of the fundamental value of fairness, then the professional conversation surrounding standards can be far more productive. We can acknowledge the flaws in standards without sacrificing the value of fairness. We can accept legitimate criticism of standardized tests without abandoning commitment to the values inherent in standards. In moving on through this book, I ask you to disassociate the pressures and unfair practices of standardized testing from the standards themselves.

POOR IMPLEMENTATION

In setting up the primary argument in his book *Motivating Students and Teachers in an Era of Standards*, Richard Sagor (a recognized cheerleader for students and teachers) acknowledges that "[i]mplementing standards-based reforms [. . .] can result in reduced opportunities for teacher creativity, personal and professional growth, and the likelihood of gaining satisfaction from one's work. Such reforms can lead [. . .] to disastrous consequences" (2003, p. 2).

In his book *Improving Schools From Within* (1990), Roland Barth states that "list logic," or the use of academic standards for educational change, seems simple, straightforward, and compelling. "Its only flaw is that it does not seem to work very well" (p. 39). He explains that "[m]ost teachers and principals respond to even enlightened lists not with renewed energy, vigor, and motivation, but rather with feelings of tedium, oppression, guilt, and anger" (p. 39). Our standards often represent for us what we should be doing, and they may remind us of the inadequacies of our teaching.

In fact, there are many schools now where teachers are required to turn in their lesson plans each week with the standards carefully written next to each activity, in order to show that every planned activity in some way meets a standard or two, a protocol so out of touch with teachers and best practices for students, I find it hard to believe. Where a teacher is supposed to come up with the time to do all that work is beyond me, but shamefully, it is a practice happening all over the country.

PRESENTATION

The standards documents themselves couldn't be any *less* like the rich, wonderful literature we share with our children on a daily basis. I'm not sure I understand why they have to be so dry. They are usually very thick, packaged in plain binders with ominous fonts screaming out such uncreative titles as, "FIFTH-GRADE ACADEMIC READING AND WRITING STANDARDS." Where is the sense in giving a document of this nature to one of the most literature-loving groups in the entire world and expecting them to be jazzed about reading it?

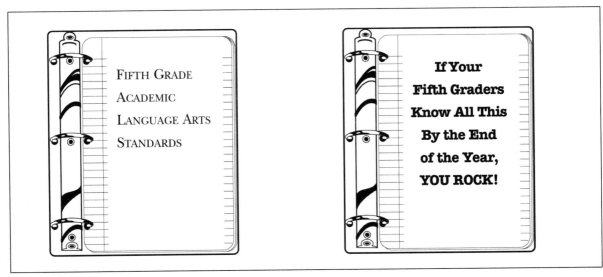

FIFTH GRADE
ACADEMIC
LANGUAGE ARTS
STANDARDS

If Your
**Fifth Graders
Know All This
By the End
of the Year,
YOU ROCK!**

Which would you rather read?

You get one of these lovely, thick documents for each major subject to be taught. Most of us can remember lugging our pile of standards to our cars after our welcome meeting that first year of teaching. New teachers learn quickly

Lesson Name: *Our Five Senses*

Unit Name: *Details! Details! Details!*

Unit Type: *Strategy* **Grade Level(s):** *K–2*

Focused Instruction: *Explain that writers use their five senses when they write. Chart the five senses. (Draw icons for each.) Use an anchor text with strong sensory detail such as I Stink! by Kate and Jim McMullan to show how authors write sensory details into their stories.*

Independent Practice: *Take students on a sensory walk. Have them draw or write things they see, smell, hear, feel, and taste while on the walk.*

Wrap Up: *Have students share with a partner what they experienced on their walk. Challenge students to state their observations in a "literary way"—how it might sound in a story such as "The sky looked as blue as my swimming pool" versus "I saw the sky."*

that hauling their standards around to meetings is a great use for the Radio Flyer they have parked in the corner of the classroom. Literally and figuratively, standards can feel heavy and overwhelming. (They don't generally present as the type of material someone would want to hunker down with under a cozy blanket by a fire, do they?)

Perhaps it is the format that turns teachers off. Standards really are just lists—lists of skills—boring to read all the way through. Many teachers make the mistake of thinking of these standards as interchangeable with a scope and sequence—what to teach in what order. They really aren't intended that way. People don't learn in a linear fashion, one skill per day, and so on. Teachers know this, which is why they may become overwhelmed when they try to make heads or tails of the standards. It is mindboggling when we try to marry this linear list to learning theory that states that children learn in a spiral fashion, constantly needing to revisit skills and build upon prior knowledge. Where do you start? Where do you end?

Tell about the things you saw, felt, heard, tasted, smelled.

Boring ☹	Exciting ☺
I saw water.	The water was gray, green, blue, always changing hue. Amber seaweed, speckled sand bubbly waves that kiss the land.
I heard a train and some dogs.	Somewhere behind us a train whistle blew long and low, like a sad, sad song. A farm dog answered the train.
We smelled lunch.	The smell of fish sticks on the grill drifted to my nose. The waffles smelled as sweet as candy and the pizza's cheese bubbled and melted.
It was cold.	I could feel the cold, as if someone's icy hand was palm-down on my back.
I tasted salt.	I taste the ocean and wonder why it tastes like tears I sometimes cry

PERCEPTION

Whenever I mention standards in my seminars, it rarely fails that I hear moans and groans from the audience, and I can hardly blame the offenders. Our standards have negative connotations for many teachers. Eye rolls, heavy sighs, and head shakes are common body language in conversations about standards. It is so easy to let the standards get the better of us. They can feel like a nuisance, a menace to the creative process, or a thief of our most precious resource—time. Teachers also like to be in charge, in control, kings of our classrooms. Standards can feel like a threat to that sense of authority.

Lesson Name: *Bad Grammar Gone "Good"*

Unit Name: *Effective Sentence Structures*

Unit Type: *Conventions*   **Grade Level(s):** *3–5*

Focused Instruction: *Review run-ons and fragments which would have been taught previously in unit. Explain that sometimes authors include run-ons and fragments in their writing purposefully. We call these intentional run-ons or intentional fragments. They are not mistakes, but rather are done for a reason. Use anchor texts to demonstrate samples of each. Discuss why an author might intentionally include these types of sentence structures in his or her writing.*

Independent Practice: *With partners, students search for intentional run-ons and intentional fragments in books. (Later students will practice using these sentence structures in their own writing.)*

Wrap Up: *Students share the intentional run-ons and fragments they found, and state what they think might be the author's purpose for including these sentence structures in their writing.*

If you find yourself in this camp, it will be difficult but worth the effort to make an attempt at opening your mind a bit more to the standards and to think of them more as a tool for planning than a hindrance. There is good in them, and using your standards for the betterment of your kids and your classroom can be empowering.

Knowledge Is Power, So Let's Get Acquainted!

Maybe you are already convinced that your standards are more of an ally to you than an adversary, but if not, spending time getting to know your writing standards may at least give you a different perspective. You may think, for example, that the standards have one very serious flaw—the standards are *finite*, and children's learning is truly *infinite*. This is true, but perhaps this is more of an opportunity for you than a problem.

Being familiar with your standards is the key to building a curriculum that meets those standards and still allows time and opportunity for your students to transcend them. When you use standards in a way that makes sense, when you plug these finite skills into units of study in writing that feel rich and appealing to you and to your students, you turn your standards document into a valuable tool. More than that, your standards become a starting point for planning, a foundation on which you will build the part of the writing curriculum that enables your students to soar beyond the standards.

We can learn a lot about our standards from the book *Enemy Pie* by Derek Munson. The main character of this book, a young boy, has a new enemy when Jeremy moves into his neighborhood. All the other kids in the neighborhood seem to like Jeremy, and this young boy finds himself missing out on great events like birthday parties because of the fact that he considers Jeremy an enemy.

The young boy's father, seeing an opportunity for his son, decides to help. He tells his son that he knows a great way to get rid of enemies: invite the enemy to the house and feed him enemy pie. So the father sets his plan in motion. As he bakes the pie, the two boys play together in the yard. The young boy soon decides that spending time getting to know Jeremy was really all that was necessary to turn things around. He soon realizes that he rather likes Jeremy, and quickly considers him a friend instead of an enemy. (Fathers can be so wise!)

Richard Sagor states, "I firmly believe that every student and teacher can come to school each day and enter the classroom excited about the challenges ahead. [. . .] The result of the standards movement—for better or worse—is in the hands of everyone engaged in the education profession" (2003, p. 1). This is a refreshingly optimistic position, and one that counters the helpless feeling many teachers have in an era marked by demands on our teaching.

THE STANDARDS DOCUMENT—IMPORTANT THINGS TO KNOW

Let's consider what we are dealing with in terms of standards. The following is information I wish had been explained to me when I started out as a teacher. You've probably been tempted, on occasion, to just sort of ignore those standards sitting over there on your shelf. Maybe you glance over in their direction every now and then to make sure they are still there. But ignoring the standards and refusing to grapple with them actually leaves you in a position of powerlessness instead of control. So, let's conquer the beast!

If you already know everything there is to know about your standards, good for you! You can skip this part.

Just Another Genre of Text

When you pick up a brochure, a travel book, or an historical fiction novel, you have expectations about that particular type of text already in your mind before reading. You have encountered these genres before in your reading life, and you know what to expect before you read. "Why is this type of writing necessary in the world?" "What do we use this genre for?" "How do we read this genre?" "Who writes this type of text and for whom is it intended?" "What should we expect when we pick up a book of this type?" As adult readers, we hardly consider these questions anymore when we read, but the answers are crucial to our understanding.

We can approach our standards the same way. You probably never encountered this genre of writing prior to entering the teaching profession. So give yourself some time to consider the standards as a new genre in your literary life, just as you would introduce a new genre to your students. Give yourself time to explore, discover, notice, and define this genre (I'll help a little).

How Are Standards Typically Organized?

State standards are all different, so they don't all follow the same format. However, there are some constants. Most standards documents will include content standards, performance standards, or both. Content standards outline the vital bits of information (e.g., identify parts of speech in a sentence),

Attention Professional Developers:

I was once asked to run a professional development session on literacy standards. After attempting to plan an outfit that wouldn't stain from all the tomatoes I figured would be hurled my way, I decided on a different approach. I dumped a whole bin full of language arts standards out onto a table of teachers. Over the growls and whimpers, I invited each of them to grab a copy and start flipping through it, writing their noticings on sticky notes and adding them to a chart called, "What We Noticed About Our Writing Standards." It started slowly, but teachers were soon writing! The conversation during this time buzzed. The room was full of "ah-ha" moments. Observations occurred all over the spectrum, from simple to sophisticated, which of course was wonderful because, like in any classroom in America, we had very diverse learners in the room.

What is important to understand is that the learning occurring during this exercise was active and critical, exactly what we hope to bring into our classrooms. Teachers were not being fed information about the standards—they were discovering the information themselves. They were saying things like, "Oh, wow . . . listen to this language here, it says that we only have to *introduce* that skill. I never knew that!" or "Every line here starts with a verb, I think that may be significant!" or "You know, this really is only enough to fill up four days of poetry, which means I can supplement the rest of this unit with other poetry-related things I really love to teach. I don't have to give up all my favorite lessons after all!"

This exercise is nonthreatening and collaborative. I highly recommend having a real look at the standards as a means for higher understanding.

skills (e.g., use the writing process to revise a piece of writing) and habits of mind (e.g., draw from own experiences to frame writing topics) that should be taught and learned in a particular year of school. Performance standards determine the degree or quality of performance students are expected to achieve in relation to the content standards. For example, if the content standard states, "Student will write in the narrative format," a related performance standard might say, "Student will publish two narrative pieces."

Some attempt is usually made to group the standards into sections. The writing standards in Arizona, for example, are grouped into strands and into concepts within the strands. The groupings for the third-grade standards are as follows:

STRAND ONE WRITING PROCESS	STRAND TWO WRITING ELEMENTS	STRAND THREE WRITING APPLICATIONS
Concept 1: Prewriting Concept 2: Drafting Concept 3: Revising Concept 4: Editing Concept 5: Publishing	Concept 1: Ideas/Content Concept 2: Organization Concept 3: Voice Concept 4: Word Choice Concept 5: Sentence Fluency Concept 6: Conventions	Concept 1: Expressive Concept 2: Expository Concept 3: Functional Concept 4: Persuasive Concept 5: Literary Response Concept 6: Research

FROM THE PLAN BOOK

Lesson Name: *Ish!*

Unit Name: *Using Mentor Texts*

Unit Type: *Process* **Grade Level(s):** *K–2*

Focused Instruction: *Read the book* Ish *by Peter H. Reynolds. Tell students that authors get ideas from other authors, and although they don't exactly copy what other authors do, their books might look "Mem Foxish" or "David Shannonish." Encourage students to read books and think to themselves, "I could write a book like this!" Demonstrate with familiar texts that have strong structures for your students to mimic. (Example: Pull out the book* Tough Boris *by Mem Fox. Review the book, and say, "I could write a book just like this! I have a dog named Cali, so maybe my book would be called* Tough Cali.*") Do this with several books. Explain that using an author's ideas is okay, but copying the words is not; each writer has to make the book his own.*

Independent Practice: *Students look through the bin of books labeled "Great Mentor Texts" that you have created for this unit. (Students can also add books they feel would make nice mentor texts.)*

Wrap Up: *Students share with a partner, showing the real mentor text, and expressing a book idea they have based on that text.*

Looked at this way, the standards aren't that intimidating! They are merely three easy-to-understand groupings of the types of skills Arizona third graders need. Each of these concepts has a list of specific subskills under it, making the list seem vast, but it's really just three simple groupings of skills. Okay, you can handle that! From this list, we can begin to see groupings that will come in handy when we start planning units of study in writing. (No performance standards are included in the Arizona writing standards.) In chapter 3 we will discuss in much more depth the types of units you might design.

Standardese—the Language of the Genre

As in any other genre, the standards documents make use of a specific type of language, and it will pay off to become somewhat familiar with it. I call it "Standardese." Standardese can be heavily dependent upon verbs, where each listed skill begins with a verb such as *determine, evaluate, conduct, add,* or *maintain.* It is much like résumé language. Standardese

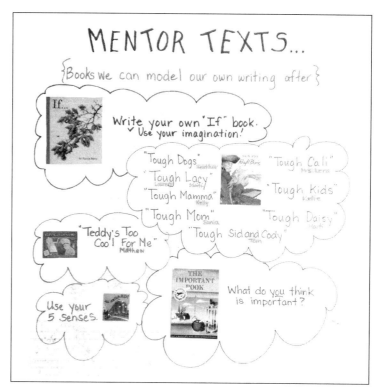

Teach your students to read like writers and to learn from their favorites and yours.

Mentor Texts With Strong Text Structure

Tough Boris by Mem Fox

It Looked Like Spilt Milk by Charles G. Shaw

My Mama Had a Dancing Heart by Cynthia Rylant

Not Norman by Kelly Bennett

The Okay Book by Todd Parr

If by Sarah Perry

The Important Book by Margaret Wise Brown

No, David! by David Shannon

Underwear Do's and Don'ts by Todd Parr

Brown Bear, Brown Bear by Bill Martin, Jr., and Eric Carle

If You Give A Mouse A Cookie (and other books in this series) by Laura Numeroff

Don't Let the Pigeon Drive the Bus by Mo Willems

Counting Kisses by Karen Katz

also tends toward the vague. "Use a variety of specific and accurate words that effectively convey the intended message" is quite imprecise, leaving the analysis of meaning up to the reader. Standardese also draws on subjective verbiage such as "relevant" and "appropriate" that leaves the determination of what exactly is relevant and/or appropriate up to you. Conversely, Standardese can at times be quite specific, particularly when discussing writing conventions, including definitive skills such as homonyms, complex sentences, characterization, plot, and figurative language. On occasion, these specific terms may be included in an accompanying glossary.

Rest assured—these interesting aspects of Standardese actually give you more wiggle room for planning curriculum!

Why Do We Have Standards, Anyway?

This may seem obvious to you, but answers vary, so let's consider. As I've said, the standards document is merely a list that outlines *what* our kids should know or perform by the end of the year. Standards are not designed to be the *how* of our teaching. This is great news! As a list, the standards can actually benefit us in several ways. Sagor (2003) believes that standards can bring both optimism and professionalism to teaching. So what are the benefits of being obligated to lists of standards?

Planning

The standards help us plan, though they don't help with the nitty-gritty planning of each and every minute of the day. Instead, they help us understand what to put in our curriculum map. The standards guide us toward biography in second grade or toward the persuasive essay in fifth grade. The standards identify for us that we should spend some time on critical book response in fourth grade or the use of the comma in third grade. The standards won't tell you how or when to go about getting your kids to experience, learn, or master the skills they list. They simply let you know that these are the skill areas for which you need to design lessons.

Many districts and schools across the country do the legwork for you in methodology. They purchase programs that tell you how and when to teach. Millions and millions of dollars are spent annually on prepackaged curricular programs. Some are highly rigid and scripted. Others leave a little more leeway for critical teaching decisions and design. Some programs are pre-

Lesson Name: *I'm a Specialist*

Unit Name: *All-About Books*

Unit Type: *Genre*   **Grade Level(s):** *K-2*

Focused Instruction: *Explain that everyone is a specialist in something. "We all have different interests, so that makes us specialists in different things. For example, I am a specialist in reading because that is a hobby of mine, while my husband is a specialist in SCUBA diving because he loves to do that and knows a lot about it. Authors of all-about books choose the topics of their books this way. It wouldn't make sense for me to write an all-about book on building rocket-ships because I don't know very much about that. If I wrote such a book, it would probably be very short and not make much sense!" Give more examples using the children in the class, such as, "Do you think Joseph should write an all-about book on farming or Emily should write an all-about book on being a dentist?"*

Independent Practice: *Students contemplate the subjects on which they are specialists, drawing or sketching a list.*

Wrap Up: *Students share their lists with a partner.*

Note: *This lesson can be adjusted for older students by focusing more on researching a topic of interest for a report.*

sented by the curricular departments as resources for your teaching; others are presented to teachers as the "script."

You may hear that the curricular programs adopted by your district are standards-based or standards-aligned, which implies that the adopted program, if followed, will meet all of your state's writing standards. The problem here is that standards are different from state to state, so although your curricular program may be aligned to some state standards, they may not be from your state. You very well may be teaching in Kansas, using a curricular program that was based on California's state standards or teaching in Oklahoma, using a program based on the language arts standards for Texas.

There is usually some attempt at making the curricular programs general enough to meet all state standards. But no matter what, your curricular programs probably will not meet all of your language arts standards. If you rely on it to do so, you will likely be omitting some critical skills listed in your state's standards for your grade level. The only way to know how well your language arts program will help you meet your state language arts standards is to compare them. To design a comprehensive writing calendar for your own classroom, you may need to fill in some gaps. Know your standards and use the curricular programs you have been given, but also think about what else your students will need in order to receive well-balanced writing instruction. Blindly following a curricular program won't guarantee you will meet all of your standards. More important, blindly following a curricular program may cheat your students of the opportunity to soar beyond those standards.

Assessment

Without getting too technical here, teachers need a way to determine whether their students are meeting the goals of their lessons. We have only two choices for assessment. We can compare our students to their peers or we can compare them to a set of standards. My preference is always to keep any sort of peer comparison out of the assessment equation. As a teacher, I have too much respect for individual students to position them in reference to their peers. Unless that child comes out on the top of the heap, the inference is that she is "less" than someone else.

I'd much rather clearly understand whether or not my individual students are meeting their curricular goals. In using a list of standards to assess your students, you can plainly see which skills are mastered successfully and in which areas your students need additional support. In *The Leader's Guide to Standards* (2002), Douglas B. Reeves

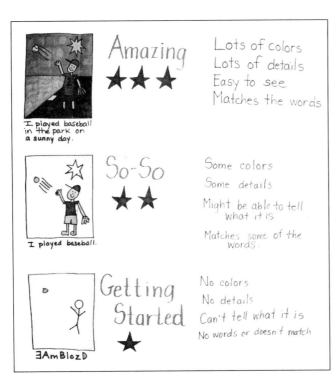

Rubrics help all students reflect and self-assess.

Lesson Name: *Illustration Rubric—A Classroom Tool That Makes My Writing Strong*

Unit Name: *Launching the Writing Period*

Unit Type: *Process* **Grade Level(s):** *K–2*

Focused Instruction: *Build upon previous lessons regarding rich, detailed illustrations by reading and discussing the book My Dog Is as Smelly as Dirty Socks and Other Funny Family Portraits by Hanoch Piven. (This book is also excellent for teaching similes.) Revisit the idea that there are many tools in the classroom that students can use independently during the writing period. Explain that these tools will help make their writing strong. Introduce a new tool: the illustration rubric (see box on page 62). Create the rubric (over 2 or 3 days). Explain that students should use the tool to decide the status of their illustrations. Explain that if their illustrations still need work, the tool can help them decide their next steps to make the illustrations "amazing."*

Independent Practice: *Students assess their illustrations using the new illustration rubric. Students add necessary elements to make their illustrations "amazing."*

Wrap Up: *Chat with class about how using the rubric is going. Ask for a few volunteers to share their experiences. What did they notice? What did they add to their picture? How did their illustrations change because of it? Reiterate that students can use the tools independently.*

states that, "The ultimate success of academic standards depends on effective educational leaders who grasp the difference between a fad and a value . . . Fads come and go, but values endure. Standards do endure, not through legislative mandates or administrative cheerleading, but because they are the fairest way to assess student performance" (p. xv).

Equity

Standards also help to ensure equity of instruction. If all teachers met their professional obligations to the state standards, then at the very least students in the same grade level all across that state would have access to the same subject matter. As we all know, schools are not equitable for a whole host of reasons too numerous to go into here, but one of the ways to begin addressing this problem is to give teachers the knowledge, support, and resources they need in order to meet and exceed their state standards. The answer does *not* lie in telling teachers what to say, what to do (and precisely when)—a strategy that virtually guarantees students won't soar above average.

In most cases, it is in our poorest communities that teachers are forced to use tightly scripted programs. The case is made that these programs are necessary in failing schools—that in these areas our curriculum has to be regulated or systematized. How backwards! These students, like all others, need the dignity of their personalities honored and celebrated at school. By scripting curriculum and tying teachers' hands, we are robbing kids in our poorest communities of their very right to exceed average by exploring and discovering new knowledge.

What If My Standards Are Just, Well . . . Really, Really Limited?

This is a definite possibility. How comprehensive do standards need to be? This question is a tough one to answer. If the standards present a brilliant and thoroughly rigorous list of objectives for a particular grade level, they would leave very little wiggle room for teacher supplementation. If the standards are too loose or general, they may not provide much of a guide for planning. So the likelihood (or at least the hope) is that your standards lie somewhere in between, providing you with a jumping-off point for mapping your year, while still giving you the wiggle room you need in order to tap into your passions and creativity and to honor the unique individuals in your classroom each year. Whatever the case, the only way for you to know how much wiggle room you have is to become familiar with your standards.

If they are somewhat limited, this can actually be a tremendous opportunity for you. You may have more chance than some others to lift your students beyond the average expectations of a standards document. When the standards are vague or minimal on a particular subject, it won't be difficult to offer more experiences that go beyond. Consider what the Arizona writing standards say about poetry for first grade:

> [Students will] participate in writing simple poetry,
> rhymes, songs, or chants. (Strand 3; Concept 1; PO 2)

That's all it says about poetry! Since poetry is by far my favorite thing to teach in first grade, I find this tremendously exciting. I know I can meet that—piece of cake! And I know this leaves me ample opportunity to supplement this unit. If I plan poetry as a three-week unit of study, I'll have plenty of time to have my kids explore onomatopoeia, simile, metaphor, repetition, personification, and imagery . . . all content well above the expectations of the standards. Also, this is content I can confidently and passionately teach.

Lesson Name: *Show and Tell*

Unit Name: *Painting Pictures With Words*

Unit Type: *Strategy* **Grade Level(s):** *3–5*

Focused Instruction: *Explain to students that great authors know the difference between showing and telling in writing. A telling sentence is when an author simply tells about a sensory detail, such as "The sky was blue that day" or "I smelled popcorn." A showing sentence shows the audience how something looked or smelled or felt, sounded, or tasted. Showing sentences paint much more vivid pictures in a reader's mind. Showing sentences put readers in the story so they can experience the event as vividly as if they were there that day too. Read some examples of showing sentences from familiar books. Discuss the sentences and what the telling sentences would have been if the author had written it that way. (Example from* <u>Owl Moon</u> *by Jane Yolen: "A train whistle blew, long and low, like a sad, sad, song" could have been written, "I heard a train.") Reveal a chart on which you have written a few telling sentences, such as "The dog was small," "I tasted the peach," and "He was nice." Together, chart alternate (showing) versions of these sentences. "The dog was the size of a peanut." "The juice of the peach tasted like the summer sunshine itself." "He fed me homemade soup when I was sick."*

Independent Practice: *Students search their own writing for examples of telling sentences. They revise these sentences, turning them into showing sentences.*

Wrap Up: *Ask each student to bring at least one revised sentence to the closing meeting. Have students share their sentences with a partner. Ask a few to share with the group.*

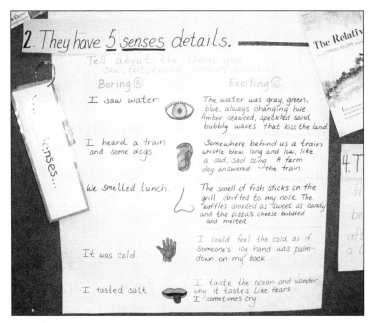

Give students concrete ways to "add detail" to their writing.

Over the course of the three-week unit, our writing wall, which showcases the learning we do within the unit, grows way beyond what the standards recommend I teach about poetry to first graders.

My students' writing always reflected above-standard learning. My poets always created stunning poems that danced and sang off the page. They wrote repeating lines that stirred emotion, imagery beyond their years, onomatopoeia that roared and zipped through the air, and sophisticated similes that played like little movies in our minds. Parents would begin to call and write with compliments. It was like magic, and yet it was no magic at all. Rather, it was the direct effect of standards-based writing instruction supplemented by a knowledgeable, passionate, and capable teacher who happens to love poetry.

Introspective Teaching

In short, our standards are only as empowering as we allow them to be. To ignore them is to give them power over us and our teaching. To become intimately familiar with them is to turn them into a valuable teaching tool. We can only be critical thinkers about curriculum if we are familiar with the standards we are obligated to teach. When a teacher arrives at a new district, she is often given a set of standards and boxes upon boxes of purchased curriculum that is meant to meet those standards. A savvy teacher is able to compare the two and to make decisions about how they stack up. Does my reading and writing curriculum meet all of my state standards? How will I help my students meet the standards not addressed in the curriculum? Most important, how will I ensure that my students are not limited by these standards? How will I encourage my students to soar above the standards?

PART 2

Teaching Above-Standard Writing in Your Classroom

The cyclical nature of teaching is one of my favorite aspects of the job. Each year, you start off refreshed and excited; your classroom is sparkling clean and everything is in place. Perfect pencils (with no bite marks), bright, unfaded bulletin board fabric, a new and hopeful class list, and a promisingly blank plan book greet you at the end of the summer.

The treadmill swiftly starts, and it is not long before you are running at full speed. By day two (because on day one your eagle-eye picked up on a few rather talkative assemblages), you have taken a blade to the perfectly taped-down desk name tags and stuck them back down several times, causing them to bubble and wrinkle. By the end of the first week, you have five to-do piles on your desk, and your student lunch monitor alerts you to the fact that the bottom of your community lunch basket has some sort of ooze in it. So starts your elementary year.

The days come and go, and you begin to tick them off on your classroom calendar. You'll have about 180 days filled with smiles and tears, parent newsletters and field trips, science experiments and parent conferences—180 days jampacked with bloody noses, "Joey's throwing up!" and "She cutted!" Each of those 180 mornings will be launched by 180 pledges of allegiance to the flag.

You'll realize you have only a meager 180 days to challenge the gifted Mairin and a measly 180 opportunities to convince Matteo and Casey that math really can be fun! You'll have a mere 180 chances to eclipse Julian's humming habit, and 180 days to pull Eric out of his safe little world where speaking is optional. During those same 180 days, you'll have to convince Frankie's dad (who greets every woman he passes in the hall each morning with "How YOU doin'?" Wink, wink) that Frankie's girl-chasing at recess must stop!

Teachers everywhere get a bit overwhelmed at the start of the year, especially when they begin to leaf through their standards documents. They'll have 180 days to visit ancient Egypt, explore three types of rock, teach the difference between a want and a need, read 8,589 books, and administer what feels like a zillion assessments. They have only about 180 chances to leave students inspired and independent, and to give them the ultimate gift of reading and writing.

Toward the end of the year, weary and exhausted, you'll crawl toward the finish line. Bleary-eyed, you'll roam the halls in a daze wondering if it will ever end, feeling sad because you know it will. "Almost there!" you'll congratulate each other in passing that final week. "Almost there!" you'll weep as you look across the room at your students, burning their images into your brains where they will stay always young and always exceptional.

During summer recess, much to the amazement of the general public, teachers continue to work. You reflect on the previous year and think. What worked really, really well? What could have been better?

In the next few chapters, we'll put our ideas into action. We'll first look at the year as a whole, carefully identifying key elements of a comprehensive writing program. We'll next go deep into a unit of study, providing opportunities to meet select standards while still including room for additional learning above the standards. We will venture into sample units of study that are designed to align with standards while allowing for students to become actively immersed in new and exciting learning. We will discuss what the writing assessments might look like for this type of teaching, and we will explore assessments as a tool for reflection and planning. Finally, we will uncover new and exciting literacies, significant in the lives of our students that may not be addressed by your writing standards. Part Two is designed to help you become skilled at lifting your students and their writing well above the average expectations set forth by your standards.

Chapter 4

The Above-Standard Year

"Which of your five senses do you think is the most important?"
—Mrs. Lera
"Your sense of humor."
—Curran, age 7

I deally, your yearlong plan for writing should do the following:

- Include lessons that ensure all students *meet* all writing *standards*.
- *Address* the *four critical skills* writers need for success—process, genre, strategy, and conventions.
- *Incorporate* opportunities for active inquiry into quality writing.

Planning your year with these goals in mind will guarantee an above-standard writing experience for your students.

Units of Study

I strongly advocate teaching through units of study. By "unit" I refer to a block of time during which the lessons you teach are focused toward clearly defined learning goals. This is not the traditional definition of a broad thematic unit, such as "Animals" or "Community Helpers," but instead a more concentrated set of lessons under a common umbrella such as "Narrative Writing" or "Being a Helpful Writing Partner."

UNITS OF STUDY SIMPLIFY PLANNING

For one thing, I think it is a much easier and much more responsible way to plan. Planning a whole clump of time around a specific purpose is simply easier. You know that struggle in the first week of school to fill every single little time slot in the plan book with an activity? In the first week, your major curriculum just hasn't gotten rolling yet, so planning the first week feels like a hodgepodge of lessons that lack coherence. But once you get into your major curriculum, your days flow better, and it becomes much easier to plan. Instead of writing the details of each disjointed activity, we can instead plan entire blocks of time (weeks, even!) around specific goals for learning.

UNITS OF STUDY GIVE INDIVIDUAL LESSONS GREATER FOCUS

Units of study also give meaning and focus to individual lessons. Designed around specific "big picture" subject matter, units keep the classroom community grounded in the learning. When you know the overarching learning goal of the next week or two, you will be more apt to plan lessons that will help you and your students meet those specific goals. "Students will learn about friendship" is not a clearly defined learning goal. "Students will produce a memoir" is clear and focused. The lessons you design to get to his or her goal will surely include the skills your students need in order to write a memoir.

UNITS OF STUDY MAKE STUDENTS ACTIVE

Units of study give students a reason to actively participate in learning. There is a team spirit, a collective ambition with expected participation around a specific objective. Students taught in units of study come to school every day with eager anticipation. They know what's coming, and they find themselves looking forward to it. Children can mentally prepare and thus participate in the learning more actively this way. The information within the unit of study envelopes students inside the classroom, and then follows them outside as well.

When children in a third-grade class are immersed in a unit of study on book reviews, for example, they begin to think like critics of literature. For three weeks or so, these children look at books differently; thinking about what is really "good" or what didn't "work" about a particular book. They read the backs of books in the library and bookstore with a more analytical eye. They "save up" information from their outside lives to bring to school, where they know they will use it. When they are reading at night, the third graders involved in this study might think, "This was a really great book. I think I'll write a review on it tomorrow during writing."

Conversely, when students come to expect that they will be presented with random, disconnected activities each day they attend school, they become passive learners, disengaged from the process. Disjointed strings of lessons don't help anchor students to the subject matter. They aren't grounded in anything real for students, so they are perceived as less relevant. Students in this type of environment learn that they can't anticipate what is to come, which may be highly unsettling to certain personalities.

The unit of study becomes a journey of sorts, where the explorers (teacher and students) begin with a thrilling clarity about the upcoming

Lesson Name: *Planning for a Publishing Party*

Unit Name: *Historical Fiction (or any genre unit)*

Unit Type: *Genre*   **Grade Level(s):** *3–5*

Focused Instruction: *Write the publishing party on the class calendar so students know when the big event will be. Explain to students that they will have to manage their time so that their piece is published and ready for the party. Suggest that as they are writing, students should make sure to include all of the important elements of historical fiction you have talked about and will continue to talk about throughout the unit, because they will be sharing their published pieces with a real audience. Together, decide who will be invited to the party, and how the newly published pieces of historical fiction will be presented.*

Independent Practice: *Students continue to work on their historical fiction pieces with an eye on time management, a sense of audience, and a renewed feeling of purpose.*

Wrap Up: *Ask students, "How is everyone feeling about the date for the publishing party? Will you all be able to make it? What are some ideas for those who feel a little nervous about not finishing on time?" Address individual concerns about making the deadline in conferences.*

FROM THE PLAN BOOK

adventure and end with a sense of having been somewhere important. Units of study in all subjects should be clearly marked on the classroom calendar, built up with anticipation, introduced with flair, communicated with par-

Lesson Name: *Derek's Smart Character Observation*

Unit Name: *Character Development*

Unit Type: *Strategy*   **Grade Level(s):** *4–5*

Focused Instruction: *"Let's look back at our chart of all the things you noticed about how an author develops characters in a story. Derek mentioned something I thought was really smart. In fact, I hadn't even planned on teaching you this, but he brought it up and I think it is really important. Derek wondered out loud that day if authors describe the characters based on people they know in real life. I got to thinking about this, and I remembered one of my favorite authors, Mark Twain, who created some of the most vivid characters in literature. Mark Twain's characters are always so real that I feel sad—like I'm going to miss an old friend—when I finish his stories. I checked on the Internet and sure enough, it was exactly as Derek said. Mark Twain used this strategy! When he made up characters, he described people he really knew. People think one of his most famous characters, Jim, in Huckleberry Finn was based on his best friend."*

Independent Practice: *Students practice describing characters based on people they really know.*

Wrap Up: *A few students share their descriptions of characters, demonstrating vivid characterizations. Guide observations through questioning: "Wow, do you feel like that is a real person? What makes you feel that way?"*

Notes: *Throughout this book, I make room for the unanticipated and very smart observations students always bring into their units of study in writing. When students are challenged to actively inquire into a new topic, questioning and noticing everything they can, they will infuse color and personality into the studies. Our students' interpretations are usually very astute and worthy of study. This lesson honors this phenomenon. Keep in mind this is just an example. This conversation can occur in any type of unit, at all grade levels.*

ents, and celebrated at the end. This becomes a ritual in the classroom and a unifying experience for all involved.

Linda Alston, a brilliant teacher and the author of *Why We Teach* (2008), also teaches through units. Her classes are alive with learning. She loves her students clearly and totally, and they know it. She ruminates that she "leaves room for that which inspires her." Of teaching through units of study, she writes: "I should also add that [my] units of study are almost always written by me and they usually go beyond the prescribed curriculum. Packaged thematic units are great, but the ones that I create around an idea that genuinely hooks me are my best" (pp. 80–82).

A unit of study also represents an opportunity for your students to show responsibility and independence when specific expectations are placed upon them. During a unit of study, your students should understand that the goal is for the whole group to learn something new together. There is a "let's all go explore" rallying cry, and students respond by helping to build an understanding of the unit topic based on their active (albeit guided) exploration of the subject.

UNITS OF STUDY GET EVERYONE ON THE SAME PAGE

Clustering lessons into units of study also enables clearer communication between you, your administrators, and parents, naturally rallying the whole team around the specific learning. Busy teachers don't always have the time to publicize play-by-play events in the classroom, but a quick newsletter outlining the course of study over the next few weeks will go a long way in terms of additional support. Most of the time, parents just need a little nudge in the direction of the right books at the library, for example, and they are happy to support your efforts at school.

Once you begin to communicate your units of study to parents and administrators, you can also communicate about your units to other staff members throughout the school. Enlist the help of your librarian, who can provide you with a bin of books to support your unit; your special education staff, who would be willing to lend additional support; and even your specials teachers who may be able to incorporate your unit focus into their lessons as well. When the whole school community is on the same page, the learning grows exponentially. (See chapter 8 for more on integrating standards schoolwide.)

TEACHING VIA UNITS OF STUDY IS SUPPORTED BY BRAIN RESEARCH

Brain research supports teaching within units of study. Susan Kovalik, an educational scholar who marries brain research with curriculum design, asserts that the most successful methodologies take into account the way

Lesson Name: *Introduction to Narrative Unit*

Unit Name: *Narrative*

Unit Type: *Genre*   **Grade Level(s):** *K–5*

Focused Instruction: *"Guess what, everyone? Today is finally here . . . the day we start our unit on narrative writing. This unit will last for five weeks, and during that whole time you will explore this kind of writing to see what it is and how you might write it yourself. At the end, we are going to invite the parents in for a publishing party. Does anyone know what narrative writing is? Well, that's okay because that is what we are going do for the next five weeks—learn what it is well enough so that we can all write our own narratives. To get us started, I put all of my favorite narrative books in this box. I'll read you one of my favorites. It's called* The Relatives Came *by Cynthia Rylant."*

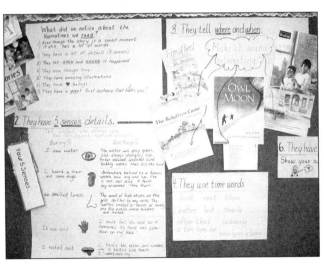

Start with a blank wall and add to it throughout the unit.

Independent Practice: *Students get time to sift through the narrative bins and make noticings about this style of writing. Students write on sticky notes and prepare to discuss their noticings.*

Wrap Up: *Chart the noticings students have about narrative writing.*

the brain processes information. Recent students show that the human brain is wired to notice patterns, and it is within these patterns that we learn new information (Kovalik & Olsen, 2001; Hart, 1983). By clustering related teaching points into units of study with a name and a purpose, we present new information in a way that best imprints the human brain.

Units of Study in Writing

In writing, a unit of study is defined as a period (one to six weeks) of purposeful, active inquiry into a writing skill, strategy, or topic. A writing unit should have a clear curricular purpose. Know your goals clearly, and tell your class at the onset. The entire community should clearly understand the purpose of the next few weeks. A unit of study in writing should be specific and focused on a particular writing genre, behavior, strategy, or tool. A unit of study in writing may be as simple as a one-week unit on comma rules or as complex as a six-week unit on expository writing.

We'll get to the actual planning of your year in a moment, but for now, envision your academic year as a series of units one to six weeks in length. You can begin to think about how you might present the information contained in your standards by simply grouping them into logical units. This approach aligns much more successfully with how we learn than an approach which simply delivers the standards day-by-day in a linear fashion where the skills are not connected to broad goals.

Take, for example, comma use. Most second-grade teachers across the country have comma use in their writing standards. Many expensive curriculum programs have taken a rather disjointed approach to this skill, incorporating isolated comma drills randomly throughout the year. The comma rules addressed by these programs are limited to those rules listed in the second-grade standards. But what if some second graders are ready to learn other, more sophisticated reasons commas are used? The programs offer no way to accommodate these students. Also, these programs don't mirror what we know about how the brain best learns (in relevant patterns). But setting up a flexible structure in which students are scaffolded as they make "discoveries" about how commas are used in real literature, gives students a greater chance of learning more and learning it with greater permanence.

DISJOINTED INSTRUCTION	UNIT-BASED INSTRUCTION
Second graders perform daily oral language exercises, practicing standards-based conventions skills in random order. Comma usage appears on days 4, 15, 67, 99, 118, 159, and 171.	Second graders participate in a two-week unit of study called "Clever Comma Use for Smart Writers." Students search through books, looking for ways commas are used. With their teacher to guide them, students chart what they notice, resulting in a group-constructed comma rules chart. Their teacher supplements their discoveries with direct lessons about each rule. Students practice their new discoveries about commas in real writing.

The feeling of the unit-based example for learning about commas is that of a group of friends going on a learning journey together to see what they can find out. The clear goal, and the one toward which all students are working, is for their own writing to grow stronger and clearer based on the new rules they are discovering about how and why commas are used.

By far, the best advantage to teaching writing through units of study is that our students become writers instead of passive receivers of information about writing. Students have lots of time within units to "try out" the new information in their own real writing.

Much to the dismay of their teachers, most students have at one time answered the parent question, "So . . . what did you do at school today?" with a shoulder shrug and a nonchalant, "nuthin'." These kids probably aren't being purposefully misleading. They really don't know. They aren't sure what the purpose of the activities they participated in was, or what the lesson they just completed was meant to teach them. Even kindergartners can benefit from our telling them exactly why they are doing something, even if the clear goal for that day is "just because it is fun!"

When you teach reading and writing through units of study, your students will instead have well-informed answers to when their parents ask them what they did at school. (Okay, okay . . . most of the time, anyway.) These kids are empowered to answer that question clearly because they

Lesson Name: *Why Did He Write It Like That?*

Unit Name: *Read Like a Writer*

Unit Type: *Strategy*   **Grade Level(s):** *K–2*

Focused Instruction: *"Writers of all kinds of books have fun with words. When we read books, we should put our writing hats on to get ideas. We can look at books and think, 'I think that looks like fun. I think I'll do that in my next piece.' I noticed something really neat in this book I think we can all do. In I Howl, I Growl Marcia Vaughan made some words big, some small, some twisty, some bumpy. She made her words look like what they mean."*

Independent Practice: *Students write, playing with words and how they write them to look like what they mean.*

Wrap Up: *Share some student work from the day. Reiterate the point that today was all about borrowing another author's cool strategy for our own writing.*

know the answer, and because they are active participants in the learning. Instead they'll proudly assert, "We're in a unit on commas, Mom. We're learning how to use them to make our writing sound smart!"

Reading and Writing: A Symbiotic Relationship

Bring to mind the natural ebb and flow of reading and writing in your own life, and you begin to understand the strength of teaching them in tandem. When planning your writing year, keep in mind that your instruction will be most effective when your writing units are logically blended with complementary reading units. Though this is a book about writing, it assumes that you are planning in such a way as to support your writing instruction with your reading instruction (and vice versa). One simply cannot exist without the other. It is essential to nurture the symbiotic relationship between these two intertwined skills. One way you can do this is to consider your reading map for the year while you create your writing map. By scheduling your reading units just a tad ahead of the writing units, you can support the important work you are doing in

Creating a Warm Classroom Climate

Optimally, your units of study should be projected through a very relaxed and informal tone similar to that which you might observe between parent and child. Lessons typically begin by tapping into a prior experience that helps children recall related information. Simply sit down and chat with your students, just as a parent does with her own children. Let plenty of support and praise accompany your message, and offer tons of encouragement toward exploration and discovery. Have fun! Ham it up! Be a storyteller. Let children see your human side. Set grand anticipation and be genuinely excited to see what your students will do. What follows is a sample exchange between teacher and students during a focused instruction lesson in a poetry unit. Note the relaxed, informal nature of the conversation.

TEACHER: Hey guys . . . check this out. This is so neat. Remember when we read that poem a while back called "Fog" by Carl Sandburg? It was in our reader. I remember Jesse read it out loud to us and we all loved it so much that we read it five more times in a row.

JESSE: Yeah! I remember!

JACOB: Oh yeah!

MICHA: Was that the one with the cat's feet?

HELEN: Oh yeah!

TEACHER: Well, today in our poetry unit, we are going to do the same thing Carl Sandburg did in his poem, because he is a really smart poet, and I feel like you can be just as smart as he is. Remember how we noticed that it was like the fog was alive in his poem? Like the author closed his eyes and imagined what it would be like if the fog was a character, and then he wrote about that? That's actually a fun thing that writers do because it is silly and powerful all at the same time. It even has a name. You want to hear what it's called when writers do that?

STUDENTS: YEAH!

TEACHER: It's called *personification* (writes word on chart).

STUDENTS: Whoa!

TEACHER: That's a very long and fancy word, but I know that you can handle it because of how smart you all are. Can you think of why it is called that?

writing by introducing various print concepts prior to asking children to perform them. For more information about planning complementary reading and writing units, see *The Complete 4 for Literacy* (2007), by my LitLife colleague Pam Allyn.

BELLE: Oh, I see the word *person* in there . . . maybe because it is like the fog is being like a person sneaking around and stuff?

TEACHER: Exactly! The fog was like a cat in that poem, but it is the same idea. *Personification* is when a writer pretends like a thing that isn't really alive is *alive*! It's so fun. It is like playing pretend. Do you all like to play pretend?

CLASS: Mmmmmm-hmmmmmm! Totally!

TEACHER: Did you know that you can play pretend with words, too?

CLASS: We can? No way! How cool!

TEACHER: One thing, though—the writer usually makes sure that the thing is acting in a way that makes sense. Like when Cynthia Rylant said that her trees held out their arms like dancers . . . remember that?

STUDENTS: Oh yeah!

EMILY: That was the book *In November*!

TEACHER: It makes sense that the trees are like dancers because that is exactly what they look like when all the leaves are off and the trees are bare. Do you think it would make sense to say that the trees snored?

JUAN: Ha ha, no that's silly. Why would a tree snore?

JILLIAN: Well, maybe if there is a hurricane!

TEACHER: Okay, well what if I said that the kite danced?

EMILY: Oh, yeah that makes sense, like if it is a really windy day and the kite was dancing around in the sky.

TEACHER: Yep, that's personification! Can you think of any more?

GIANNA: I know! The wind kissed my cheek.

TEACHER: Yowza! How in the world did you get so smart? That's a great one!

BRIAN: The water tickled my toes.

TEACHER: Oh, man, I *knew* it! You *can* handle this . . . this is going to be soooo great today. Okay . . . practice by turning and telling a partner one personification idea. Then, go back to your desks and try personification in your poems. This is another way that writers make their poems great, and now you know how to do it! Go play pretend with words! I can't wait to hear what you write today.

Toward Planning an Above-Standard Year

At this point, you're likely thinking, "Standards? Yearlong planning? I see where this is going! **RUN**!" Trust me, I understand your trepidation. I've been there. But what most teachers realize immediately when I start working with them in this way is that we are looking at planning, a traditionally burdensome task, in a whole new way—in a way that feels smart, clear, organized and well, dare I say . . . easy?

First, don't panic. I won't ask you to toss out your old ways of doing things, nor will I suggest you NOT use adopted curriculum to which you are obligated. You are already teaching in very strong ways that honor your standards. So although I may reshape a thing or two or add something here and there, I won't ask you to rethink all of the wonderful teaching you've done to this point. Just the opposite; I hope to honor those glorious passions you have about teaching, and the ways you have already helped your students meet their standards.

Made of tag board with a moving arrow, the "pie" is an excellent visual aid for your students.

Secondly, I ask you to keep your mind open to the idea that the standards can be a useful planning tool. (I realize this step may take a little mental muscle!) With just a few simple steps, you will begin to see your year clearly and masterfully. You will discover that meeting your standards is not just doable, but it is also possible in a way that will allow additional time to ultimately encourage your students to write well above them—in a way that is

Lesson Name: *Using "The Pie"*

Unit Name: *Launching the Writing Period*

Unit Type: *Process*   **Grade Level(s):** *K–5*

Focused Instruction: *"I want to show you this round chart here that we'll be using a lot during writing time this year. It is called The Pie and it will help us know exactly what we are all supposed to be doing at each stage of our writing hour. The nice thing is that this arrow here moves around, so we can point it at the right section of the pie to show what we are doing. That way, everyone knows what they should do without being confused or asking." Explain each of the three stages of the writing period (focused instruction, independent practice, and wrap up) and what is expected of each of the students at each interval.*

Independent Practice: *Have fun rotating the arrow around the pie so that your students can act out the appropriate behaviors at each interval.*

Wrap Up: *Discuss what you noticed about your students' behaviors.*

enjoyable for you and your students. You will create a year of writing that feels truly strong; a year of writing that makes you feel proud to teach.

Now that we've discussed the importance of planning units of study in writing, let's start planning. Next, we will consider a few steps that, if followed, will assist you in planning an above-standard year.

STEP ONE: GET FAMILIAR WITH YOUR WRITING STANDARDS

If it is possible, try this first step with a partner or group. The questions included in this section make wonderful discussion points. Since the ultimate goal is to start noticing ways the standards may be sensibly grouped into units, another set of eyes may lend additional perspective to how your writing skills may be clustered together. If you can work with your own grade-level team, you will be well on your way to successful collaboration as you plan your year of writing.

As I said before, knowledge is power. Flip through your writing standards and start getting to know them. You need to have a clear vision of what your standards say, because it will be up to you to not only teach them all, but to fill in any gaps in writing skills you may have if your standards feel limited or out of balance. As you read through your standards, try to take the focus off the individual skills and think more globally about what your standards obligations are. Ask some questions that will begin to guide you toward logical groupings of writing skills.

- What is the format of your writing standards? How is the information grouped? Are there section headers that help you see groupings?
- Do your writing standards include academic standards or performance standards or both?
- Do your writing standards feel full and comprehensive, or are they rather brief? Do your writing standards give you enough to fill an hour a day for the year? How much autonomy do you think you will have in filling your year?

The ultimate goal here is to start noticing the ways your standards may be sensibly grouped into units, because ultimately you will be planning units of study, and you will be clustering your standards into the units you design. The next few steps will help you more specifically with this task.

STEP TWO: PUT YOUR STANDARDS ASIDE FOR A MOMENT AND GET TO KNOW THE FOUR ESSENTIAL SKILLS ALL WRITERS NEED

Remember the three goals for planning your year listed at the beginning of this chapter? The second was to plan a year that addresses the four critical skills mastered by all successful writers. So what are these four specific skills we must make sure our writers develop? The reason we put the standards aside for this discussion is that we have to leave room for the fact that your standards may not address all four. We'll discuss that important point in a moment. For now, let's get to know these four critical components of writing success:

- Knowledge and understanding of the writing **process**
- Knowledge and understanding of a variety of **genres**
- Knowledge and understanding of many writing **strategies**
- Knowledge and understanding of the **conventions** of written language

The Complete 4™: Process • Genre • Strategy • Conventions

Why *these* four categories?

My wonderful colleagues at LitLife poured years of research, expertise, and experience into identifying the four abilities that all successful readers and writers possess. Pam Allyn and colleagues determined that all successful writers have a healthy grasp of each of these four sets of skills—The Complete 4. With the identification of these four skill sets, teachers can now easily see a comprehensive year as a healthy balance of all four. Each of the Complete 4 writing skills is so inherently important and interdependent that a year doesn't feel complete or comprehensive without attending to them equally.

Process

Strong writers have an excellent grasp of the processes of writing. Process skills are those healthy habits of mind successful writers demonstrate. These are the tools that writers need in order to think critically and write independently.

> [P]rocess [lessons] ensure that students have the tools they need to delve into all other areas of learning to read and write—from nuts and bolts practicalities, such as where to actually go in the room during certain lessons and where to store materials they will need for their reading and writing to much more sophisticated interactions and instruction in the upper grades as to the nature of conversation between teacher and student, and the best modes of communicating when working with groups or with partners (Allyn, 2007, p. 38).

No topic is too small for a process lesson. Time spent on what to do if a pencil breaks is time well spent. But from there, process lessons can become much more highly developed. The complex skill of conducting a successful editing partnership would also be categorized as a process skill.

Genre

Strong writers understand genre. The genre skills are related to the ability of a writer to effectively identify and write within specific styles of text. Effective writers understand the unique features of each of the genres, identify the distinctive purposes for the different types of writing, and can select the correct genre for the purpose of a piece of writing. Writing standards that address the crafting of personal narratives, report writing, and poetry, for example, are genre standards. In many standards, the genres are called writing "applications."

Strategy

Strong writers utilize various writing strategies. In writing, strategies are those specific techniques writers employ across all genres of text that lend greater quality to writing. Strategies are needed before, during, and after the actual writing takes place. Before writing, a strong writer plans. She considers the organizational structure that will best support her message. She will read similar texts critically in order to gain understanding of her project. Strategies make writers planful and decisive about their writing. During the writing itself, a successful writer employs various strategies as well. Purposeful use of specific imagery tools such as simile, metaphor, and vivid details qualifies as a writing strategy. In fiction, story elements such as strong character development and theme are also topics for strategy instruction. Strategies such as these help strong writers create brilliant texts that exceed expectations. Strong writers employ additional strategies after drafting a project. Effective writers are well aware of the benefits of revision and editing and make habitual use of them to improve the quality of the writing product. For these writers, the acts of writing, revising, and editing occur simultaneously, as the use of them is genuine and artful.

Conventions

Finally, strong writers benefit from familiarity with and use of proper grammar and writing conventions. A triumphant grasp of the often complicated rules of written language comes gradually and requires instruction rooted in real writing and plenty of practice to become natural and creative.

Successful writers know their punctuation, grammar, vocabulary, and spelling very well, but they aren't slaves to them, bound by rules and stunted by the very thought of being "wrong." Instead, pride comes to these writers through competence. Strong writers often tinker with language playfully. But in order to do this, a writer must have an initial grasp of the "rules" of our language in order to fine-tune drafts in ways that add deeper meaning to text.

I don't mean to imply that great writers ignore the rules—just the opposite: they are so familiar with them that they can masterfully tweak the conventions to create deeper meaning.

To give our students the same chance at grammar use, we have to do more than teach it. Just as we do with the other three qualities of successful writers, we must give our students grammar competency. It isn't enough for our students to simply place punctuation marks in the right places on a worksheet when grammar aptitude can be such a valuable skill for writers.

Teaching the Conventions With Purpose

Shel Silverstein artfully played with conventions, a common practice of many accomplished authors. Consider the number of times you've been cautioned not to start a sentence with a conjunction such as *and* or *but*. You may have even passed this rule on to your students once. In his book *The Giving Tree*, Shel Silverstein starts almost every single sentence with *and* or *but*. As many writers do, Shel Silverstein made an intentional decision to start his sentences with conjunctions.

The Complete 4 Units of Study in the Teaching of Writing

Writing is a subject area and requires a curriculum. Teaching inside units of study helps you to organize your thinking and maximize your teaching time. The Complete 4 abilities demonstrated by successful writers should be included in a well-balanced year. The chart on page 86 shows examples of the types of units you might teach in each category.

STEP THREE: CATEGORIZE YOUR STANDARDS IN THE COMPLETE 4 CATEGORIES

Ideally, your writing standards will include equal portions of each of these four skills, but more than likely, they will not. Since your ultimate goal is to design a year that creates strong, effective writers, you must understand whether your writing standards are providing enough of each of the Complete 4 skills to ensure total writing success. In this step, you must view your writing standards through the lens of the Complete 4.

The chart on the next page shows the types of individual skills that may

PROCESS	GENRE	STRATEGY	PRINT AND CONVENTIONS
• Creating a writing community (ARCH) • Developing a writing identity • Stamina • Pacing • Fluency • Conferring • Peer conferring • Partnerships • Text clubs • Text talk • Topic choice • Making plans and setting goals • Storytelling • Independence • Mentors • Tools of a writer • Content area writing • Writing about reading • Assessment and reflection • Revision • Writing under timed conditions • Finding writing ideas • Developing writing ideas • The Four Prompts (Observe, Wonder, Remember, Imagine) • Techno-literacy	Narrative: • Narrative/fiction • Memoir • Personal essay • Short story • Play • Folktales • Mysteries • Historical fiction • Fantasy • Science fiction • Series • Biography Persuasive nonfiction: • Persuasive essay • Book Blurbs/Reviews • Literary essay/criticism • Editorial • Debate • Speech • Feature article Informational nonfiction: • News article • Essay • Biography • All-about book • How-to text • Question/answer book Poetry Letters Picture books Standardized tests	• Rereading • Activating schema • Making connections • Visualizing • Determining importance • Written inference • Planning • Interpretation • Critical analysis • Character development • Story elements • Retelling • Summarizing • Note-taking • Research • Theme study • Author study • Organizational structures • Revision • Writing to a prompt • Studying craft strategies • Close study of an anchor text • Reading like a writer	• Concepts of print • Grammar • End punctuation • Pausing Punctuation • Linking punctuation • Dialogue • Capitalization • Fluency and phrasing • Syntax (sentence structure) • Sentence types/variety • Parts of speech • Editing • Spelling strategies and resources • Conventions as a craft tool • Paragraphs • Roots, prefixes, suffixes • Word origins

appear in your standards and their corresponding Complete 4 categories. As you read through your writing standards, begin to think about which of the four qualities (process, genre, strategy, and conventions) each skill addresses. Is the skill a conventions skill? Is it a process skill? Is it related to genre? Is it a writing strategy? In many cases, the standards will already be grouped this way in at least one of the categories. California's standards, for example, include a grouping of skills called "writing applications," which is the grouping that refers to the genres. If your standards aren't already grouped in this way, you can easily categorize them yourself.

Use the Complete 4 Standards Analysis Tool (Appendix, page 196) to categorize your writing standards. Read through your writing standards and place them into the appropriate categories. With all of your standards in one place, categorized in this manner, you will be able to see a clear picture of whether or not your standards are well balanced. Once you have categorized your standards, you'll have a simpler (and much more visual) way to analyze them.

Step back and take a look at how your standards fall into the four categories. In which of the Complete 4 categories do the bulk of your standards lie? Are your columns equal? Is one category bulging with the weight of many standards? Are any of the categories omitted or only rarely mentioned? The answers to these questions will help you balance your year.

As an example, let's look at California's grade-four writing standards in their written form:

WRITING STANDARDS—CALIFORNIA, FOURTH GRADE

WRITING

1.0 Writing Strategies

Students write clear, coherent sentences and paragraphs that develop a central idea. Their writing shows they consider the audience and purpose. Students progress through the stages of the writing process (e.g., prewriting, drafting, revising, editing successive versions).

Organization and Focus

1.1 Select a focus, an organizational structure, and a point of view based upon purpose, audience, length, and format requirements.

1.2 Create multiple-paragraph compositions:

    a. Provide an introductory paragraph.

    b. Establish and support a central idea with a topic sentence at or near the beginning of the first paragraph.

    c. Include supporting paragraphs with simple facts, details, and explanations.

    d. Conclude with a paragraph that summarizes the points.

    e. Use correct indention.

1.3 Use traditional structures for conveying information (e.g., chronological order, cause and effect, similarity and difference, posing and answering a question).

Penmanship

1.4 Write fluidly and legibly in cursive or joined italic.

Research and Technology

1.5 Quote or paraphrase information sources, citing them appropriately.

1.6 Locate information in reference texts by using organizational features (e.g., prefaces, appendixes).

1.7 Use various reference materials (e.g., dictionary, thesaurus, card catalog, encyclopedia, online information) as an aid to writing.

1.8 Understand the organization of almanacs, newspapers, and periodicals and how to use those print materials.

1.9 Demonstrate basic keyboarding skills and familiarity with computer terminology (e.g., cursor, software, memory, disk drive, hard drive).

Evaluation and Revision

1.10 Edit and revise selected drafts to improve coherence and progression by adding, deleting, consolidating, and rearranging text.

2.0 Writing Applications (Genres and Their Characteristics)

Students write compositions that describe and explain familiar objects, events, and experiences. Student writing demonstrates a command of standard American English and the drafting, research, and organizational strategies outlined in Writing Standard 1.0.

Using the writing strategies of grade four outlined in Writing Standard 1.0, students:

2.1 Write narratives:

    a. Relate ideas, observations, or recollections of an event or experience.

    b. Provide a context to enable the reader to imagine the world of the event or experience.

    c. Use concrete sensory details.

    d. Provide insight into why the selected event or experience is memorable.

2.2 Write responses to literature:

    a. Demonstrate an understanding of the literary work.

    b. Support judgments through references to both the text and prior knowledge.

2.3 Write information reports:

    a. Frame a central question about an issue or situation.

    b. Include facts and details for focus.

    c. Draw from more than one source of information (e.g., speakers, books, newspapers, other media sources).

2.4 Write summaries that contain the main ideas of the reading selection and the most significant details.

WRITTEN AND ORAL ENGLISH LANGUAGE CONVENTIONS

The standards for written and oral English language conventions have been placed between those for writing and for listening and speaking because these conventions are essential to both sets of skills.

1.0 Written and Oral English Language Conventions

Students write and speak with a command of standard English conventions appropriate to this grade level.

Sentence Structure

1.1 Use simple and compound sentences in writing and speaking.

1.2 Combine short, related sentences with appositives, participial phrases, adjectives, adverbs, and prepositional phrases.

Grammar

1.3 Identify and use regular and irregular verbs, adverbs, preposi-
tions, and coordinating conjunctions in writing and speaking.

Punctuation

1.4 Use parentheses, commas in direct quotations, and apostrophes
in the possessive case of nouns and in contractions.

1.5 Use underlining, quotation marks, or italics to identify titles of
documents.

Capitalization

1.6 Capitalize names of magazines, newspapers, works of art, musical
compositions, organizations, and the first word in quotations
when appropriate.

Spelling

1.7 Spell correctly roots, inflections, suffixes and prefixes, and sylla-
ble constructions.

After categorizing the California fourth-grade writing standards on the
Complete 4 Standards Analysis Tool (Appendix, page 196), we can look at
these same standards more clearly.

The Complete 4 Standards Analysis Tool (Completed for California, Grade 4)			
PROCESS	**GENRE**	**STRATEGY**	**CONVENTIONS**
Students: • show they consider the audience and purpose.	Students: write narratives [that]: • relate ideas, observations, or recollections of an event or experience. • provide a context to enable the reader to imagine the world of the event or experience.	Students: • write clear, coherent sentences and paragraphs that develop a central idea. • progress through the stages of the writing process (e.g., prewriting, drafting, revising, editing successive versions). • Select a focus, an organizational structure, and a	Students: • write fluidly and legibly in cursive or joined italic. • use simple and compound sentences in writing and speaking. • combine short, related sentences with appositives,

continued

PROCESS	GENRE	STRATEGY	CONVENTIONS
	• use concrete sensory details. • provide insight into why the selected event or experience is memorable. Write responses to literature [that]: • demonstrate an understanding of the literary work. • support judgments through references to both the text and prior knowledge. Write information reports [that]: • frame a central question about an issue or situation. • include facts and details for focus. • draw from more than one source of information (e.g., speakers, books, newspapers, other media sources). Write summaries that contain the main ideas of the reading selection and the most significant details.	point of view based upon purpose, audience, length, and format requirements. Create multiple-paragraph compositions [that]: • provide an introductory paragraph. • establish and support a central idea with a topic sentence at or near the beginning of the first paragraph. • include supporting paragraphs with simple facts, details, and explanations. • conclude with a paragraph that summarizes the points. • use correct indention. • use traditional structures for conveying information (e.g., chronological order, cause and effect, similarity and difference, posing and answering a question). Students: • quote or paraphrase information sources, citing them appropriately. • locate information in reference texts by using organizational features (e.g., prefaces, appendixes). • use various reference materials (e.g., dictionary, thesaurus, card catalog, encyclopedia, online information) as an aid to writing. • understand the organization of almanacs, newspapers, and periodicals and how to	participial phrases, adjectives, adverbs, and prepositional phrases. • identify and use regular and irregular verbs, adverbs, prepositions, and coordinating conjunctions in writing and speaking. • use parentheses, commas in direct quotations, and apostrophes in the possessive case of nouns and in contractions. • use underlining, quotation marks, or italics to identify titles of documents. • capitalize names of magazines, newspapers, works of art, musical compositions, organizations, and the first word in quotations when appropriate. • spell correctly roots, inflections, suffixes and prefixes, and syllable constructions.

continued

PROCESS	GENRE	STRATEGY	CONVENTIONS
		use those print materials. • demonstrate basic key-boarding skills and familiarity with computer terms (e.g., cursor, software, memory, disk drive, hard drive). • edit and revise selected drafts to improve coherence and progression by adding, deleting, consolidating, and rearranging text.	

(Adapted from California Language Arts Standards, Grade 4)

In this example, the largest grouping of skills falls within the strategies category. The rest are divided between the genre and conventions categories. The process category is greatly underrepresented, so fourth-grade teachers in California would need to design writing process lessons to include in their curriculum to ensure balance across the skills. (Occasionally process standards may be found outside of the writing standards, in another area of the literacy standards, or perhaps even in behavioral standards.)

The idea is that you will want to make sure your students receive a healthy balance of all four of the qualities demonstrated by successful writers. Since you will be planning your year first and foremost using the standards, this step helps you see the gaps—those areas of misalignment between a comprehensive, balanced year and your state writing standards. By categorizing your standards skills in this way, you are beginning to develop the familiarity that you need to plan your year. This is an excellent foundation for your above-standard year.

STEP FOUR: IDENTIFY UNITS OF STUDY FROM YOUR NEWLY CATEGORIZED STANDARDS

Now that your standards are grouped into the Complete 4 categories (process, genre, strategy, and conventions), you are ready to embark upon the most enjoyable part of this planning—identifying the units of study you will teach over the course of your writing year. This is the best and most

Lesson Name: *Fun With Apostrophes*

Unit Name: *Punctuation*

Unit Type: *Conventions* **Grade Level(s):** *3–5*

Focused Instruction: *Tell students that improperly placed apostrophes can change the meaning of a sentence to something unintended. Read the book* The Girl's Like Spaghetti *by Lynne Truss. Discuss the different meanings implied by the different placement of the apostrophe in each sentence. Review the main ways to use an apostrophe (contractions, single possessive, plural possessive). Chart apostrophe rules.*

Independent Practice: *Students write "Lynne Truss"–style sentences—two alternate versions of a sentence with the apostrophe in two places, creating two different meanings.*

Wrap Up: *Post sentence pairs around the apostrophe chart.*

creative part of the planning.

The idea here is to start to extract the big ideas that you feel could make strong one- to six-week units of purposeful study. Look at your standards within their Complete 4 groupings. It is here that you will begin to notice clusters of standards that relate to one another. In the conventions category, for example, you may notice that eight of your standards skills relate to comma rules. You could plan a unit of study on comma rules for writing. You may notice that there is a large grouping of standards in your process category that relate to writing partnerships. You might, then, plan a unit of study on writing collaboration. You may notice that there are no standards at all in your process category. You might then plan a unit of study on how authors choose topics, a process skill you feel is crucial to the success of your students.

> ### Goals for a Comprehensive Year of Writing:
>
> - Meet all of the writing standards.
> - Teach all of the Complete 4 Writing Skills equally and comprehensively.
> - Allow for active inquiry into the world of writing.

You may also notice that certain skills in different Complete 4 categories can complement one another. For example, there may be only three short skills in your genre category that relate to expository writing, but there are several standards in your process category that relate to the organization of writing pieces. Based on your experience, you know that teaching organization is impossible if not rooted in the actual type of writing that must be organized. So, you might plan a unit of study on report writing with a focus on organizing this type of text. This way, you teach your genre standard for expository writing and process standards for organization in one unit.

This is the most inspired part of the planning because it allows you to be imaginative. It is actually enjoyable to sit back and think deeply about how you might cluster these seemingly random skills into exciting units that would be pleasurable for both you and your students to spend time in, particularly if you carry out this step with a group of colleagues. "Students will include correct ending punctuation 90 percent of the time" is so dreary compared to a block of time planned for a unit of study called "Stop Signs" that includes a

FROM THE PLAN BOOK

Lesson Name: *Mind the Stop Signs*

Unit Name: *Ending Punctuation*

Unit Type: *Conventions*   **Grade Level(s):** *K–2*

Focused Instruction: *Tell your students you are going to share one of your very favorite books. You just love this story. Read Yo! Yes? by Chris Raschka, but read it ignoring all ending punctuation, in a very flat voice all words running together. Don't show pictures. Ask your students if they liked the story. When they speak up about how they couldn't understand it, tell them that's because you forgot to read all the ending marks. Make the point that when writers forget their stop signs and when readers forget to read them, the story is very confusing. Read it again with voice inflections for ending punctuation.*

Independent Practice: *Students write with attention to including stop signs.*

Wrap Up: *Chart the three ending punctuation marks, including the reasons they are used.*

giant corresponding red hexagonal bulletin board with a period, exclamation point, and question mark on it. The possibilities really are endless!

As you begin to think about the main topics of your writing units, there are several things to consider that will help you cluster your standards into the units you will teach.

Unit Type

Each unit you teach will be categorized as a process unit, a genre unit, a strategy unit, or a conventions unit so that you can keep an eye on whether you are planning a variety of units that address all four categories of writing skills equally. By planning units that balance these four categories of skills, you will guarantee that your students receive instruction that will develop their aptitude in all four areas of writing proficiency.

Though I speak of a unit being identified by its type, it is possible (in fact probable) that some of your writing units will address more than one of the Complete 4 categories, which will be a way for you to meet many of your standards within one unit (and thus a way for you to make the most of your time). For example, you may design a genre unit on poetry that will also include strategy lessons on poetic devices. It is, however, essential for you to be clear about the main focus of your unit so that you can plan a balanced and complete year.

Unit Length

How much time will you need to teach a particular unit of study? A writing unit can vary in length depending upon the focus and type. Ideally, you will have a variety of units, some short and some longer, moving the year along at a nice clip to sustain the attention of your video-generation students. You may teach a four-week process unit at the beginning of the year to launch the writing routines. You may teach a one-week conventions unit to review a specific punctuation mark. Whatever the units you choose, try to vary the lengths.

One influence on unit length is the number of your standards and skills you can comfortably fit in the unit. The key is to strike a balance between including enough skills to create a rich and worthwhile unit filled with related lessons, but not so many as to create a lack of focus. The skills you include should relate in a logical way and should scaffold the big idea of the unit.

As I look over the Arizona state writing standards for second grade, for instance, I see that one probable unit of study for Arizona second graders would be a genre unit on narrative writing. I notice that the standards for narrative writing in this case are quite narrow, so I begin to think about narrative writing, and what other skills I can also include in this unit. Which of my standards could I include with narrative writing that would contribute positively to the teaching of this genre? I look over the standards and find some that relate to the use of author's voice, which I know would complement the narrative genre nicely. I decide that I could cluster the subtopic of voice in a unit on narrative writing. The use of voice in students' narrative texts would surely strengthen the quality of their writing during this unit of study.

A second-grade teacher in Arizona can combine the standards that address narrative writing:

> Student will write a narrative that includes a main idea based on real or imagined events, character(s), and a sequence of events.

with the standards that address voice in writing:

> Student will utilize voice, which will: vary according to the type of writing, but should be appropriately formal or casual, distant or personal, depending on the audience and purpose; show awareness of the audience through word choice and style; and write text that is expressive, individualistic, engaging, and lively.

By combining these concepts into one unit, the obligations to teach narrative writing in second grade are met in a way that gives students the edge in creating quality narratives. Even more advantageous, when the vague concept of voice (an extremely difficult concept to teach in isolation) is rooted in a genre, it is much more easily understood and performed. Students will more easily grasp the idea of writing "text that is expressive, individualistic, engaging and lively" if they are given clear instruction in techniques they can actually use to help make their text expressive, individualistic, engaging, and lively.

Lesson Name: *Great Beginnings That Hook the Reader*

Unit Name: *Narrative Writing*

Unit Type: *Genre*   **Grade Level(s):** *K–5*

Focused Instruction: *Explain that readers will decide quickly whether they want to continue to read a story. A great beginning sentence can really "hook" a reader and pull him into your narrative piece. Read (while hiding the book covers) examples of excellent beginning sentences from familiar books. Have students identify the books they are from. Suggest that students can borrow an idea from the list if they change it a little bit.*

Independent Practice: *Students experiment with great beginnings in their narrative pieces*

Wrap Up: *Ask a few students to share excellent examples of beginnings that hook the reader.*

Major and Minor

Remember that pivotal time in your life when you had to commit to a major in college? Just when you thought you had it all figured out, they asked you for a minor and you had to commit all over again.

We can apply the idea of major and minor within our units of study as well. The major is the big idea of the unit, the main topic being addressed. The minor then supplements that idea. You

Great Leads That Hook the Reader		
BOOK	AUTHOR	BEGINNING
Owl Moon	Jane Yolen	"It was late one winter night, long past my bedtime when Pa and I went owling."
The Big, Big Sea	Martin Waddell	"Mama said, 'Let's go!' so we went."
Sam and the Lucky Money	Karen Chinn	"Sam could hardly wait to get going."
Walk Two Moons	Sharon Creech	"Gramps says that I am a country girl at heart, and that is true."

may, for example, teach a genre unit on the persuasive essay and include a strategy minor on summarizing. In this way, you meet several objectives at once. You teach your requisite persuasive essay, but you do so in a way that feels purposeful and strong, since summarizing (also on the standards) is a skill that will strengthen the persuasive essay. Conversely, you teach your requisite lesson on summarizing, but you do so in a way that gives this skill purpose by anchoring it to the persuasive essay.

Desired Outcomes

Once you have identified the big ideas from your standards that you feel will be strong topics for your units, you will also need to pinpoint specific desired outcomes for the time spent within the unit. "Nonfiction writing" for example, is an excellent topic (or big idea) for a unit of study, but "nonfiction writing" is not narrow or focused enough to guide the objectives within a unit. It is better to narrow the focus of nonfiction to a mode of nonfiction that is grade-level appropriate. Think about why you will spend time in this line of study. What do you want your students to be able to do or to know or to produce at the end of this unit? Answering these questions will help you give purpose to every lesson you plan within your unit.

If the big idea of your unit will be on newspaper articles (genre), for example, the desired outcome might be that your students will write an outstanding newspaper article that includes the major elements of a news story. If the big idea of your unit will be revision (process), your desired outcome might be that your students will rework a previously written poem to include imagery.

STEP FIVE: IDENTIFY YOUR SUPPLEMENTARY UNITS OF STUDY

In the next chapter, we will explore the inner workings of the teaching that goes on within the unit and we will discuss the ways in which you can supplement the work your students do within the units themselves. For now, let's entertain the idea that you can add whole units to your year that may not be in the standards at all, or that may be in other content area standards. Let's look at several reasons for adding units to your year.

An Important Question to Consider as You Read Through Your Standards

"Is this skill best taught as a whole unit itself, as part of a unit, or should I really be teaching and revisiting this concept all year long?"

Everywhere I go, teachers ask the same questions, which I find illuminating. Just like kids are the same all over the world, so too are teachers. One common (very thoughtful) question I hear is whether the specific skill is big enough for a whole unit, small enough to be part of a unit, or broad enough to be taught and revisited all year long.

The answer to this is one of those "yes-but" responses. As with most things in life, this isn't that simple. *Yes*, it is true that some concepts need to be presented only once for all students to grasp, while others need frequent re-examining. But, because so much of this teaching depends on tapping into prior knowledge and upon making daily deposits into the common-knowledge bank, and because the teaching occurs in a relaxed and natural state, you will (by design) frequently revisit previously taught concepts. You will do this in your focused instruction lessons, your conferences with students, your wrap-up sessions, and even during the natural impromptu conversations that occur between you and your students. In short, revisiting past concepts is a fundamental part of this type of teaching. You'll be revisiting the concepts that make up the collective whole of the writing knowledge in your classroom, and on such a regular basis, that it isn't necessary to plan reviews because they are built in.

Balance

At LitLife, we suggest that a well-balanced writing year would be divided equally between the four essential writing skills.

Writing Processes	Writing Genres
Writing Strategies	Writing Conventions

A balanced and comprehensive year of writing includes a healthy balance of all critical skills.

What if my standards are clearly *not* divided into equal parts like this?

Your standards are likely *not* divided neatly into these categories. In fact, it is quite likely that your standards feel out of balance. By simply supplementing your year with the areas that are missing or too limited in your standards, you can design a balanced year of writing for your students. If your writing standards don't include much in the way of writing strategies, include a strategy unit. If your writing standards don't mention any genres, pick one you love and design a unit around it! Look back at the Complete 4 table on page 86. This chart can help you design units for areas that are lacking in your writing standards.

The ideal writing year includes equal time devoted to each of the four major writing skills, but your standards are not concerned with time. Your standards can help, but they won't tell you how much time to spend teaching each skill. It is feasible (in fact, very likely) that once you plan units that meet all of your writing standards, you'll have some wiggle room, because you will cluster many of your complementary standards together into your units. Try to balance your time equally between the Complete 4 skills. If you aren't able to devote the exact prescribed amount of time to each of the four major writing skills, try at least to come close.

Traditions

Another reason to add supplemental writing units to your year is that (as we discussed in chapter 1), there may be deeply rooted traditions in place at your school that you would like to continue to teach. I wholeheartedly advocate including these exciting events in your year! I worked with a teacher once who dearly loved her yearly tradition of writing letters to nursing home patients. We worked this activity (which was once an isolated social studies lesson) into a unit of study on personal letter writing. In doing this, the teacher kept her favorite lessons intact, combined science and social studies instruction, and met writing standards all at once.

Literary Passions

Most writing teachers have passions about the literary world, and another great justification for including a supplemental writing unit into your year is that you just really love teaching a certain thing. Maybe book-blurb writing isn't mentioned in your standards, but it is absolutely, hands down, one of your favorite things to teach. Keep your expectations high and go for it! Those subjects we're most passionate about usually make for our strongest lessons because of the energy with which we deliver them. There is no sub-

Book Boxes

Dear Parents,

Please help us create a special place for our books by student authors.

Directions:

1. Use an empty cereal box, and cut it in half like the picture. ⟶

2. Decorate the bottom half of the box creatively. You can use wrapping paper or contact paper to cover it. Please include your child's name and a photograph.

These special boxes will contain all of the wonderful writing pieces your child writes throughout the year.

Thank you,

cut here

Enlist the help of parents or make these book boxes at school. They make an excellent container for books students publish throughout the year. Hang them on the wall for an impressive display.

stitute for teacher enthusiasm. A teacher who is both informed and passionate about a topic will bring it to life in a classroom.

In second grade, my brother had a bearded, Birkenstock-wearing teacher who was really into science. His room smelled of critters and over-ripe experiments. He ran a hands-on room and his students were completely enchanted. My brother still talks about him and the interesting things he learned in that class. (This is the same brother who later majored in bio-medicine in college and sent fruit flies up on the Space Shuttle Discovery so that he and his team could observe how its immune system was affected by zero gravity!)

Who are you as a writer? Who are you as a reader? Identify your literary passions and bring them into your writing year. Most lessons delivered by a passionate and knowledgeable teacher make an impression that lasts a lifetime.

Free Cycle

As you identify your units of study for the year, you may also want to include a few free cycles. A free cycle is a one- to two-week blank spot on the calendar. I purposefully sprinkle a few of these throughout the year so that I can fill them in later in response to unanticipated events during writing instruction. As we all know, no two school years are the same, and pre-planning an entire year makes it difficult to react genuinely to the unforeseen events that inevitably arise when dealing with children.

During the year, you may find that you need to add a review unit because you've noticed that the class as a whole hasn't quite grasped something. You may also wish to add in a unit simply because a nice opportunity presents itself. One year, my class spent a week writing letters to a student's uncle who had recently been deployed to Iraq. These units bring the community together, honor the natural human experiences of the individuals sharing the classroom, and help writing time seem sincere.

Test Preparation

Another supplemental unit you may consider including is a unit on standardized test writing (or writing to a prompt or writing under timed conditions). Though I don't advocate "teaching to the test," writing to a prompt is another valid genre that students need to master. After all, that's how they'll be tested in writing for most of their educational career. I think it makes great sense to teach this skill within a unit of study. Let me be clear that a well-balanced year of strong and authentic writing instruction, the type we have been discussing thus far, will surely prepare your students for success on writing tests. Still, our students deserve to know what these tests are, what the readers look for, and how to go about comprehending the prompts and writing successfully within this genre. When we share this information with our students, they will be better able to apply all the strong writing techniques they have learned within a testing environment.

STEP SIX: SCHEDULE YOUR NEWLY IDENTIFIED WRITING UNITS IN YOUR YEAR

Now that you have carefully identified the writing units you wish to teach, the next step is to plan when you will teach them. We teachers are amusingly wired to the school calendar. When a business professional says "at year-end," like most people, they are talking about December 31. Not so for a teacher. To all teachers across the country, December 31 merely means "almost to the half-way point."

We think in terms of chunks of weeks separated by vacation days, and we tend to plan our activities with this in mind. We are also probably more in tune with the seasons and holidays than most professionals. Can you imagine a police captain saying, "I think it would be best to plan our partner strategy meeting in February, because that's friendship month and Valentine's Day, and all?"

Consider some scheduling influences as you think about where you might place these newly conceived units on your curricular calendar.

Time of Year

As you place your units around the year, you'll need to keep in mind appropriateness of timing. To begin the year, you'll want to introduce the writing time with a process unit that addresses appropriate behaviors and expectations for writing. A great way to end your year is to teach another process unit on reflection. The placement of the units in between will be influenced by many factors. Holidays and other school events could predicate the timing of a writing unit. Splitting a five-week unit across winter break isn't optimal, for example, so you'll want to schedule longer units in between vacations where you have plenty of uninterrupted time. You should also consider the teaching going on in science, math, and most important, reading. Clever teaching of related subject matter can lend strength to the year. I always scheduled my poetry unit in February, right before our school poetry contest. I scheduled my expository writing unit in spring when we were studying the life cycles of animals. My narrative unit was usually scheduled in October when we were still getting to know one another and focusing on families.

Place your units the best you can around the year. Relate them the best you can to the other teaching you will have going on in other subjects. Try your hardest to maneuver around the holidays and breaks. And after all that, realize that none of it will be perfect. You'll have a fire drill on the opening day of one of your units. You'll forget about an assembly, or you'll realize later that your animal report unit would have been great if you'd

Lesson Name: *My Writing Strengths*

Unit Name: *Reflections*

Unit Type: *Process*   **Grade Level(s):** *3–5*

Focused Instruction: *Tell students that one of the most important things writers do is to think deeply about themselves as writers. "After a whole year of writing, you should know your writing skills pretty well now. What are your greatest strengths as a writer? Are you a good planner? Do you write really vivid stories? Do you have strong voice in your writing? Do people come to you for help with illustrations? We all have strengths and it is worthwhile to know what they are."*

Independent Practice: *Students take time to look through their portfolios, noting their writing strengths on a "My Writing Strengths" page (Appendix, page 202). Students also chat with others, as their friends' perceptions of their writing strengths may be eye-opening for them.*

Wrap Up: *Lead a discussion with students about their writing selves. Ask, "Are you stronger as a writer than you were at the beginning of the year? How will these strengths help you next year?"*

taught it *after* the zoo field trip. And remember one wonderful quality of our profession: we get to clean up at the end of the year and start all over again the next, fixing and refining all of those things we wish to change!

Tools for Planning the Above-Standard Writing Year

At the back of this book, I have included an appendix that will assist you with the steps mentioned in this chapter. Be sure to use this when you are walking through the various steps in this chapter. You are well on your way. Although the identification and planning of a year full of writing units may feel somewhat intense at first, it gets easier. The more familiar you become with your standards and with the way your students receive writing instructions, the more natural it becomes. This process will grow to be one that you actually enjoy (really!) because it places you, the professional, at the helm. You will design curriculum that helps you answer the question "Are you meeting your writing standards?" with a resounding "You betcha!" You will design curriculum that challenges your students in ways that you know will be of interest to them and that will enable them to explore and celebrate new knowledge in addition to those standards. And you will design curriculum about which you are exceedingly passionate. Finally, you will see that your writing units may change from year to year, as you learn and grow and develop new interests as well.

Chapter 5

The Above-Standard Unit

"If you don't know where you are going,
you'll end up someplace else."
—*Yogi Berra*

Many of the teachers I've met across the country have interesting travel stories. It seems that teachers, as a whole, enjoy distant adventures and often will find creative ways to see the world. When you're lucky enough to plan a vacation away from home, you are faced with a few major decisions right off the bat. First, you'll need to discuss what type of vacation you want. Will you travel to a foreign place to learn about its history, people, and culture? Will you travel to your hometown to catch up with friends and family? Or will you sneak away to a quiet locale simply to rest and relax for a while?

The type of vacation you desire will affect the next two big decisions: locale and duration. Three weeks in Bali may well serve your longing for an exotic education. Four days in your hometown may well serve the purpose of catching up with far-away loved ones. A week on a beach in Belize may be exactly what you need to recharge your batteries.

Once the big decisions are made, you can then start getting into the nitty gritty details of your days. What will you do once you're there? Keeping in mind the purpose of your journey, you'll start to plan the activities you'll engage in during this focused and relatively brief time in your life. For the educational Bali trip, you'll book a quaint room in Ubud, reserve seats at a Kecak dance performance and a guided tour of Goa Gaja. For the trip to your home town, you'll phone friends and family and schedule your visits with them. For the Belize vacation, you'll simply book a *casita* on the beach and start amassing the books and magazines you'll read that week.

Imagine planning your daily vacation activities before you know why or where you are going. In terms of planning, this doesn't make any sense. Yet at times as teachers we may find ourselves falling into the habit of planning daily activities without knowing where we are going, why we are going, or how long we'll need for the journey. When it comes to planning writing instruction, it's only once we know why we'll embark on a specific unit of study and how long we'll engage in that study, that we can then begin the task of planning the meaningful activities that will fill our days within the unit itself. Whether our unit of study is one week or six, the days we have within that unit are very brief, so making the most of them is critical.

Setting the Stage—Building the Daily Structure That Supports the Work

Just as there are certain non-negotiables on any trip, there are non-negotiables that should be established in your classroom writing period that will remain constant. Establishing certain routines with regard to writing will give your writers stamina so they will be able to take full advantage of the work they will do within the units you design for them. These are those things we as writers "just do" to stay healthy and nourished throughout the writing experience. Instead of considering whether or not you should include these activities, your choices lie in where, when, and how you will incorporate them.

STAGES OF A UNIT OF STUDY

The four stages of a unit of study (immersion, identification, guided practice, and commitment) will provide the first part of our flexible framework. You and your students will be able to enjoy an ample amount of flexibility and choice within this framework, but these stages will guide those choices and help to lend some much-needed structure to many of the decisions you and your students will make along the way. As you plan, keeping these specific stages in mind will help you ensure that you are designing a focused period of study that will give your students the maximum opportunity for meeting standards and subsequently exceeding them.

Immersion

During the immersion stage, the first stage of a new unit, you and your students will literally immerse yourselves in the primary subject of the unit. This is an introductory time, a questioning time, and a time to get everyone's minds swimming with the sights and sounds of the topic of study. You will lay the groundwork for the new topic by introducing it, and you will structure the learning by then placing the appropriate tools in the hands of your students so that they can go investigate it. During this very active stage, your students will read, discuss, think, and write.

Give students easy access to excellent examples of the genre you are studying.

If you are starting a new genre unit, you'll give your students a brief introduction to the new genre, and then you'll turn them loose on a basket full of books of that genre. If you are beginning a new unit on a convention, you'll introduce the new convention and then you'll set your students to searching literature for examples about how that convention is used. Immersion is all about jumping in and exploring. As teachers, we simply structure the play by gearing it toward the unit's topic of study.

In the immersion stage of a genre unit on persuasive writing, students would

Poetry
some smart things
We've noticed...
"observations"

- They are usually all about one thing.
- They are shorter than other genres.
- Tons of sparkly words are packed in.
- They are meant to be read over and over.
- The words "sing" off the page like a song.
- The lines stop so there is a lot of white space.
- They don't always have to rhyme.
- They describe the 5 senses.
- They use showing sentences, not telling.

Let students notice what they can about the genre.

explore samples of persuasive texts, talking about and noticing unique aspects of this style of writing. In the immersion phase of a process unit on developing writing ideas, you might help students explore the ways writers get their writing ideas by visiting the Web sites of famous authors, reading books by authors about their writing experiences, or speaking directly to writers about

> **What did we notice about the Narratives we read?**
> 1) Even though the story is a small moment it still has a lot of words
> 2) They have a lot of details (5 senses).
> 3) They tell WHEN and WHERE it happened
> 4) They move through time.
> 5) They have amazing illustrations
> 6) They have ♥ feelings
> 7) They have a great first sentence that hooks you!

Chart student observations.

Lesson Name: *Introducing the How-To Genre*

Unit Name: *Functional Texts—How To's*

Unit Type: *Genre*   **Grade Level(s):** *K-2*

Focused Instruction: *"Today we are starting a new unit on a kind of writing called functional writing. Functional writing is writing that tells someone how to do something, so we'll just call it How-To writing. I gathered up a bunch of How-To books and put them here in this bin. There are cookbooks that show how to cook certain things and craft books that show how to make things. These kinds of books are quite different from storybooks and nonfiction books. I'm going to give you some time to explore these books today. Think about them a lot, and how they might be different from other kinds of books."*

Independent Practice: *Students explore the How-To books, noticing their unique qualities.*

Wrap Up: *Chart what students notice about How-To books.*

Notes: *Possible noticings for future lessons include: a title that tells what you will make, a "you will need" or materials section, clearly explained steps in order, a picture for each step.*

how they get ideas. During the immersion stage in a strategies unit on successful beginnings, you and your students could search through books, noting the interesting ways authors lead readers into their texts. During the immersion stage of a conventions unit on quotation marks, you and your students might spend a few days exploring different texts and noticing how quotation marks are used in print.

When you start a new unit, you'll begin with a list of teaching points you hope to get across to your students during the unit. Instead of delivering these teaching points directly, watch as your students begin to flesh them out during immersion. For example, if strong dialogue is one of your teaching points for a narrative unit, you can wait until you hear a student say, "I discovered that there is a lot of talking in narratives" and build on this observation.

Of course, the teaching points derived from your standards are not optional, so although most of the time the students will naturally uncover these specific teaching points during immersion, some gentle coaxing may be in order if it appears your group may miss one of the concepts you wish to teach. Don't be afraid to act a bit. Respecting your place within the group of explorers, you might say something like this: "Hey guys, I noticed something, too! May I add something to the list? As I'm looking though these biographies, I noticed that they always seem to include the reasons why the person is important, or something the person did to change our world somehow."

Though your students will be busily mining out the standards during the immersion stage, the stronger outcome of this stage is that they'll make more

STANDARD	SAMPLE ACTIVITY FOR IMMERSION PHASE OF A UNIT OF STUDY
"Explain the meaning of literary works with some attention to meanings beyond the literal level." (New York ELA, Standard 2, Speaking and Writing, Elementary Level)	Explain that some books have "life lessons" that teach us something. Use *The Empty Pot* by Demi, pointing out that this book reminds people about the importance of honesty. Students then explore the classroom library, searching for books with strong "life lessons" in them. Students discuss the books and their corresponding "life lessons" when they find them.

discoveries than you ever planned for—ever even thought of. This is where this sort of teaching leaps above the standard requirements. You'll keep an eye on those standards, and the other teaching points you chose to include, but you'll also welcome the chance for your students to learn much, much more when they are free to bring their own curiosity into the unit.

During immersion, the group senses that together you are setting out to discover all there is to know about a certain writing topic chosen by you, the teacher. You are part of the group, too, as you work alongside your students to help them discover and notice the teaching points you've planned for them. This collective feeling of discovery sets a positive and active tone for the rest of the unit.

Identification

As the group enjoys some success in the immersion stage, noticing and exploring different aspects of the unit topic, you'll start to feel a shift. You will feel a need to step in as their teacher and refine things a bit further. This is the time to do it. The identification stage is where you will do most of your direct teaching, and where you will explicitly teach the skills you have selected for the unit. Students, having been empowered to go forth and investigate during the immersion phase, will begin to develop vague understandings, and it will be up to you to step in and help them further refine their discoveries.

Much of the identification stage will involve your naming and explaining the smart observations your students are making. If, during a genre unit on narrative writing, a group of students has noticed that this style of writing often includes words and phrases such as *then* and *next* and *after that*, you'll tell your students that these are called "transition words." You'll explain that using transition words is important to narrative writing because they help the events move through time. Together, you and your students will make a chart of transition words and display it prominently in the room.

The identification lessons in a unit are defined by naming things—most often the very "things" or teaching points you planned for the unit. During a process unit on planning, you might give your students a graphic organizer to guide their planning. During a strategy unit on word choice, after students have noticed that reading a story is "like watching a movie in your head," you would explain that authors use sensory details to bring the story to life. During a conventions unit, after hearing students notice specific uses of a punctuation mark, you would name and explain the rules governing its usage. These activities are designed to bring the class community toward a collective definition of specific writing skills.

STANDARD	SAMPLE ACTIVITY FOR IDENTIFICATION PHASE OF A UNIT OF STUDY
The student evaluates his/her own writing and the writing of others [by] respond[ing] constructively to others' writing. (Texas ELA, standard 19B, Grades 1–3.)	Explain that writers don't write alone. Professional writers have editors to help them with the writing process. Explain the term "constructive criticism." Enlist the help of a student to demonstrate what constructive criticism looks and sounds like during peer conferring.

During the identification phase of your units, your classroom walls start to bloom. As you record your new learning on charts, graphs, and illustrations, your bulletin boards begin to fill with the evidence of your teaching. Any person who walks into your classroom after this stage of the unit can see exactly what your class is learning at that time. For those of you who must display your standards and how they are being met, this is a wonderful way to fulfill this requirement. And since the learning within your unit will be well above standard, your walls will broadcast this as well.

With most focused instruction lessons, you will add reference charts to your writing wall.

Guided Practice

Now it is time for your students to practice. After immersion, and the subsequent identifying of various new aspects of writing, it is time to give your students the guided activities they need to commit these new skills to memory. Guided practice enables your students to put their newfound knowledge into practice in their own writing. Guided practice is the most important phase of the study, and for the students, a very active one. During this phase of the unit, you will work alongside your students, coaching them along in their new pursuits.

This is the time to show your students how. To help your students write engaging leads, you might explore and chart the ways authors of some model texts wrote their engaging leads. To help your students build writing stamina, you might ask your students to write for five minutes longer each successive day. To demonstrate note-taking, you might model how to create an outline. To help your students get past a spelling road block, you might make a chart entitled, "What to Do When You Can't Spell a Word."

The guided practice period of your study is the time for you to wear your coaching hat. Just as a baseball coach works alongside his players, demonstrating techniques and then carefully observing his athlete's use of

Lesson Name: *Turtle Talk*

Unit Name: *Spelling Strategies*

Unit Type: *Conventions*   **Grade Level(s):** *K–2*

Focused Instruction: *"We have been adding spelling strategies to our chart so that when you get stuck on a word, you don't have to stop and sit there for a while and waste time. So far we have 'Look at the Word Wall' and 'Ask a Friend.' Today we are going to add one called 'Turtle Talk.' Turtles talk rrrr–eeee–aaaa–llll–yyyy ssss–llll–oooo–wwww–llll–yyyy llll–iiii–kkkk–eeee thththt–iiii–ssss. So they can hear each and every letter they have to write down. If you get stuck on a word, just pretend you are a turtle and say it really, really slowly to yourself so you can hear the right letters."*

Independent Practice: *Students try turtle talking the words they can't spell.*

Wrap Up: *Ask "Who used Turtle Talk today? Did it work? What word was it? Let's all try to turtle talk that word."*

those techniques, so too will you demonstrate and carefully observe how your students are picking up the skills. Practice is the most important learning time for athletes and writers alike.

Since the skills you are asking your students to practice are both standards-based and outside the limited realm of the standards (skills that were "discovered" during immersion), guided practice also becomes a time for your students to soar above and beyond the average expectations set forth in the writing standards. Because you are not limiting your lessons to only those skills mentioned in the standards, but you are guiding your students toward additional points you feel are important and you are honoring the unexpected discoveries made by your students, you are encouraging your students not to be restricted by average expectations.

California writing standards for second grade state the following:

> Students will write brief narratives based on their experiences:
> - Move through a logical sequence of events.
> - Describe the setting, characters, objects, and events in detail.
> (English—Language Arts Content Standards for Public Schools, Grade 2, writing, 2.1 a,b)

During the guided practice phase of a unit based on these standards, you could design lessons that encourage your students to practice the following in order to meet these standards:

- Moving events through a sequence
- Developing the setting (time and place)
- Describing the problem and solution

You might also wish to include lessons you deem important to this line of study such as:

- Including internal events (thoughts and feelings of characters)
- Helping your students develop more engaging main characters by including the internal thoughts and feelings the main character experiences in addition to the external details occurring during the event itself
- Developing life lesson or theme
- Helping your students include a moral or lesson to their story to increase the depth and scope of the narrative

You might also include lessons in this study that directly respond to the discoveries made by your students about narrative writing:

- Writing attention-grabbing beginnings
- Closing the story with a bang
- Creating vivid characters
- Using *like* or *as* in descriptions

With these simple additions to this otherwise standards-based unit of study, we push our students way beyond normal expectations. We push them just a bit higher by responding to their own natural curiosities about the subject matter.

STANDARD	SAMPLE ACTIVITY FOR GUIDED PRACTICE PHASE OF A UNIT OF STUDY
Use a thesaurus to identify alternative word choices and meanings.	In the computer lab, on a Smart Board or other comparable device, the teacher demonstrates how to use the electronic thesaurus on the word processing program. Students practice editing for word choice using the thesaurus.

California English–Language Arts Content Standards for Public Schools, Grade 5, Writing, 1.5

Commitment

The commitment phase of a unit is critical because it is in this final stage that your students will be held accountable for the newly gained knowledge or skill. You will ask them to demonstrate their acquisition of the new skill, and to commit to using this new knowledge going forward. The idea here is to get your students to understand that the learning that takes place within a unit of study is expected to be brought to the world outside the writing period, even outside school.

During this portion of the unit, students are asked to record or discuss their newly acquired skills and to reflect upon ways in which these new skills might help them in future literary work. In a kindergarten process unit establishing writing routines, students discuss how the charts on the walls can help any time they feel stuck. In a third-grade strategy unit on editing and revising, students note that enlisting the help of an editing partner can help spot problems. In a fifth-grade prompt-writing study for test preparation, students discuss the benefits of citing supporting evidence. Students may record their reflections individually in notebooks or collectively on charts.

STANDARD	SAMPLE ACTIVITY FOR COMMITMENT PHASE OF A UNIT OF STUDY
Ideas and Content PO 1. Use pictures that convey meaning. PO 2. Use pictures with imitative text, letters, or recognizable words to convey meaning. PO 3. Use labels, captions, or picture descriptors to expand meaning.	At the end of a unit, students invite their parents in for a publishing party during which they share their published stories. Students also share their own understandings of the narrative genre with their parents. After the party, the stories are placed in the classroom library.

Arizona Academic Content Standards for Language Arts, Strand Z, Writing, Kindergarten, Concept 1, Performance Objective 1, 2, 3.

DURING THIS STAGE OF THE UNIT:	THE TEACHER IS . . .
Immersion	An Equal Member of the Group
Identification	A Lead Teacher
Guided Practice	A Coach
Commitment	A Facilitator

STAGES OF A LESSON WITHIN A UNIT

And so it is that your units will follow this specific format. Yet what will the individual days look like within the unit? You have probably already started to get a taste for this. An above-standard day follows a flexible framework as well. Like the unit itself, the daily lesson benefits from a structure which supports the learning for the day.

Whole/Small/Whole

Your daily lessons will include three defined activities: a focused instruction lesson, independent practice, and a wrap up. This follows a "whole/small/whole" pattern. During focused instruction, the class meets as a whole. For independent practice, the students disperse into the room for solo or small-group work. The class comes back together again for the wrap-up session.

Omitting any of these three phases of your daily lesson could weaken its impact. Regardless of the stage of the unit you happen to be in at the time, all daily lessons should follow the whole/small/whole pattern. The whole/small/whole pattern eventually becomes so routine (and so effective) for both you and your students, you'll find yourself following it in other subjects without even planning to do so.

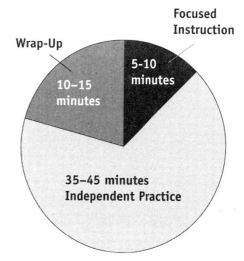

Wrap-Up

Focused Instruction

5-10 minutes

10–15 minutes

35–45 minutes
Independent Practice

● **Lesson Name:** *Planning Your Response*

● **Unit Name:** *Writing Under Timed Conditions*

● **Unit Type:** *Process*   **Grade Level(s):** *3–5*

● **Focused Instruction:** *"Smart test-takers use the writing prompt to guide their thinking during planning time. You want to be sure that when you are planning your piece of writing, you are answering all that is asked of you. Let's take a look at a sample question and break it down." (Read sample question a few times slowly, modeling the creation of a bubble chart to plan for an answer).*

● **Independent Practice:** *Students plan a response to a practice question by creating a graphic organizer such as a bubble chart.*

● **Wrap Up:** *Students share their planning process in small groups so that they benefit from hearing how others planned a response to the same question.*

FROM THE PLAN BOOK

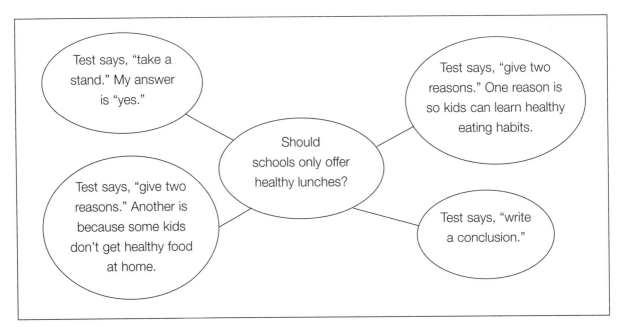

Strategy lessons can teach students methods for organizing and test-taking.

Focused Instruction

Focused Instruction is the first portion of your daily lesson, when you address the class as a whole. Your students may be gathered in front of you on the carpet, piled all over couches and flopped on pillows, or sitting at their desks, but they are all focused on you and your message. Focused instruction is meant to be short (5–10 minutes) and can be delivered in a variety of ways. Use any creative means you can to connect with your students to deliver the information. I'm a big believer in a casual, relaxed tone, so be yourself and talk to your kids genuinely, with respect and interest.

Deliver a Strong Focused Instruction Lesson

- Tell an engaging story.
- Tell about your own writing experience.
- Solicit a group solution to a problem.
- Model.
- Point out a specific technique used successfully in an anchor text.
- See what professional authors have done.
- Act it out.
- Sing it.
- Draw.
- Use a student or student's writing as a positive example.

The focused instruction lesson is meant to connect with all the other lessons in the unit, so tap into background knowledge and set the stage for the next lesson as well, where appropriate. Use the support that surrounds this one small piece of the entire unit.

Independent Practice

Independent Practice represents the bulk of the writing period (30–40 minutes), and gives your students the opportunity to take on the new knowledge you have designed for them—the teaching points you have selected from the standards and beyond. These periods represent the nucleus of your writing program. Your students will skip off from the focused instruction lesson ready to try something you've just discussed. It is during this time, a time when all children are behaving as real writers, that most of the impact of your writing instruction will take hold. Your students will grow increasingly independent.

Independent practice is also a time for you to actively participate in the process. Pam Allyn writes, "[Independent practice] is where you can monitor, observe, witness, participate in, and celebrate the successes and challenges of your work and the work of your children" (2007, p. 174). This is the time you will confer with your students individually or in small groups to push their learning even further. Conferring will enable you to know your writers intimately. By engaging in genuine conversations with your students about their writing, you will become extensively familiar with their abilities. This means that you will be able to reinforce the teaching points that need extra instruction and supplement with additional teaching points when appropriate. Struggling writers will benefit from specific,

Independent practice enables your students to use new concepts and strategies in their writing.

Some Comic Relief From a Student Writing Conference

In a conference with Darius, I noticed that he wasn't really picking up on the *oa* spelling pattern. Darius was an excellent speller, and was already incorporating all of the spelling patterns we'd studied into his writing, so I took the opportunity to go beyond the standards and talk about the *oa* combination, which is not specified in the first grade standards. Darius clearly needed this skill for the level of writing he was doing.

"Let's talk about this *oa* spelling pattern, Darius," I suggested. "I noticed that you're coming across of lot of words with the long-*o* sound and need to learn this new combination. It comes up a lot in writing."

"Okay, cool," Darius said excited to be getting an advanced lesson.

"You already know that the long-o sound can be made with the bossy *e*, like in *tone*, right?" I asked.

"Oh, sure, Mrs. Lera. I learned that a long time ago," said Darius.

"Okay, well you can also make that sound by combining the *o* and the *a*, like in *foam*," I explained.

"Oh, that's neat," Darius said.

"Okay, can you think of a word that has the *oa* spelling pattern in it?" I asked.

"Moany," Darius stated.

"Moany?" Hmmm. I don't know that one. Can you use it in a sentence?" I asked.

"Yeah. Doctors make a lot of moany!" Darius replied.

guided help in troublesome areas, but all writers will move forward because as you confer with them, you will quickly notice opportunities to push beyond the standards when and where appropriate.

When I invite educators or parents into a classroom where independent practice is taking place, I usually get the same reaction. Adults are astounded by what appears to be a busy group of quiet young children totally engaged in writing.

Independent practice tends to be quieter than you'd imagine a group of 25 kids could ever be. It has that "busy hum" about it, where the students are truly engaged in what they are doing. Instead of clinging onto their teacher or disruptively practicing headstands, engaged students operating in a flexible yet structured environment are making independent decisions and supporting one another.

As you look around a classroom during independent practice, you'll see students comfortably writing in nooks around the room. You'll see kids carefully contemplating pieces of writing and diligently creating detailed illustrations. You'll see students holding up pieces of writing to the charts on the walls and children working in groups and pairs. Even in kindergarten, students can be expected to show increasing independence during this time.

I can't, however, stress enough how much teaching goes into making your independent practice look and feel as I have described. These things don't magically happen. This is why the process units (particularly the launch unit at the beginning of the year) are critical to teaching the proper behaviors during writing time. It is in the process units where your students will develop their identities as writers. These lessons will support the independent behaviors of your students. Expectations should be carefully laid out, and students should be guided inward and challenged to act as problem solvers when writing gets tough. In schools where this teaching takes place in every classroom, though, the amount of time spent in the launch units decreases because the expectations during writing carry over from year to year.

Process units teach students how to behave like writers.

A process lesson can teach the differences between "writing talk" and "recess talk."

Wrap Up

During the wrap up portion of the lesson, the class comes back together to meet as a whole again, addressing the same topic covered during the focused instruction lesson. This reconvening enables the community of writers to review the new skill and to commit in such a way as to keep everyone accountable to the new skill. Wrap ups are quick and simple. Questions like "How did it go today?" or "Ashley, I noticed you did an incredible job crafting awesome

Most students adore being asked to share during wrap up.

showing sentences. Would you mind sharing them with the class today?" may be all that is needed to drive the point home.

Lesson Name: *Questioning Your Readers*

Unit Name: *Book Blurbs*

Unit Type: *Genre* **Grade Level(s):** *3–5*

Focused Instruction: *"Today we are going to continue our work on book blurbs. I noticed that many of your favorite blurbs start with questions. I think the book blurb writers do this to hook you in immediately. Questions are strong and they are directed right at you, the reader, so they capture your attention." Read some examples of blurbs that start with questions.*

Independent Practice: *Students write a blurb for a favorite book, starting it with a strong question.*

Wrap Up: *Have a few students share their blurbs with the class.*

Planning a Unit of Study—Defining Key Elements

Now that you have an understanding of the type of support that should be in place in your class that will sustain the above-standard teaching you will do, it is time to plan your first unit of study. Although the structures of an above-standard unit and a day in the above-standard framework may be somewhat fixed, the planning of the key elements for your study will offer you the flexibility to get creative and to use your professional judgment.

Your first step is to select the writing standards you will cluster into one unit. You are looking for standards that complement one another, that have a common theme, or that you feel you can bring together in a way that makes sense.

Let's take a look at an example. I will walk you through planning an above-standard writing unit based on the fourth-grade writing standards in California (California English–Language Arts Content Standards for Public Schools, Grade 4, writing, 1.5–1.9). For this unit, our completed unit planner would look like this:

Above-Standard Unit Planner

STANDARDS TO BE ADDRESSED BY UNIT
Research and Technology
1.5 Quote or paraphrase information sources, citing them appropriately.
1.6 Locate information in reference texts by using organizational features (e.g., prefaces, appendices).
1.7 Use various reference materials (e.g., dictionary, thesaurus, card catalog, encyclopedia, online information) as an aid to writing.
1.8 Understand the organization of almanacs, newspapers, and periodicals and how to use those print materials.
1.9 Demonstrate basic keyboarding skills and familiarity with computer terminology (e.g., cursor, software, memory, disk drive, hard drive).

Complete 4 Category to Be Addressed by unit: process genre strategy conventions

Unit Major: Tools to Aid Writing   **Unit Minor:** Computer as a Writing Tool

Unit Name: Using Writing Tools to Help Us Craft Informational Articles

continued

STANDARDS-BASED UNIT GOALS	
Students will	
1. Include information from outside sources in articles (standard 1.5).	8. Use the almanac as an aid to writing (standard 1.8).
2. Give credit to the sources used (standard 1.5).	9. Use newspapers and periodicals as an aid to writing (standard 1.8).
3. Navigate outside sources to search for information (standard 1.6).	10. Use computer as a tool for writing, editing and publishing (standard 1.9).
4. Know what reference tools are available for writing (standard 1.7).	
5. Use the dictionary and thesaurus (standard 1.7).	
6. Compare hardcover encyclopedias and online encyclopedias (standard 1.7 with teacher preference).	
7. Search the Internet for information that will aid writing (standard 1.7).	

TEACHER-CHOICE UNIT GOALS	
11. Determine the validity of information found on the Internet.	
12. Understand that people can be tools for writing because we can gather information by interviewing them.	
13. Understand that experts in their field can offer information.	
14. Use photographic illustration as a tool for clarity in writing.	

STUDENT-CHOICE UNIT GOALS	
(To be added during the unit)	

Unit Length Four Weeks (20 lessons)

Unit End Product(s) Students will discuss with a partner how they will use writing tools for future projects. Students will use writing tools to write and publish a magazine article.

This unit planner has been carefully completed with attention to standards and with allowance for additional learning beyond the standards to take place. Let's now take a look at each section of the unit planner.

STANDARDS TO BE ADDRESSED BY UNIT

I have included five standards under the research and technology section of the California fourth-grade writing standards. I feel as though I can plan a strong unit of study based on these standards. I know that I can plan a unit that will not only meet these standards, but one that will give me a chance to teach a few things I think are important (and are related to the common thread of technology and research). I will also allot some time in this unit for my students to explore the various tools available to them as writers.

IDENTIFY THE COMPLETE 4 CATEGORY TO BE ADDRESSED

The first key element for you to identify during your planning stage is the type of unit you intend to plan. Going back to the Complete 4 categories of successful writing skills (page 86), will your unit be a process unit focusing on a writing behavior? Will it be a genre unit highlighting a specific genre of text? Will it be a strategy unit focusing on a specific writing craft? Or will it be a conventions unit focusing on a certain rule of print?

It is important to clearly define the unit type because unit type will determine the kind of lessons you subsequently plan. You must know what you are trying to accomplish with each unit of study before you can plan what to teach. You have to keep your goals in mind so that each of your lessons carefully and efficiently pushes your writers toward those goals. If the goal of a particular unit of study is lifted directly from your standards, you can plan lessons that will help ensure that your students meet those writing standards. If a particular unit of study is based on a need for balance in your writing instruction, you can plan lessons that help develop a vital writing skill that was only ambiguously covered in your standards. If your class and your schedule can afford an additional writing unit beyond what is mentioned in the standards, you can plan lessons accordingly for that as well. The ultimate goal is to plan a comprehensive writing curriculum, so sticking to the specific purpose of each unit keeps your writing instruction balanced and ensures that you have taught all four essential skills: process, genre, strategy, and conventions.

In our fourth-grade example from California, it is clear that a strategy unit would be most effective here, because the standards addressed revolve around the use of tools to aid writing. In a strategy unit we can help our students use specific tools that will not only boost their writing skills during this unit, but will also carry over into subsequent writing once our students are familiar with using these resources.

SELECT YOUR MAJOR AND MINOR

As I mentioned in chapter 3, your unit major is the main focus of study for your unit. Your minor will complement your major and can enrich the teaching of the major. By writing a minor into your unit of study, you will make more efficient use of your time. Every teacher has at some point complained that she just doesn't have enough time to teach all of the things she is being asked to cover. Designing units of study with two interrelated points of focus is one answer to the time question.

Including a minor in your study could also help you to cover more standards in a more purposeful way. Anchoring these lessons to activities that are related to a major course of study gives them purpose in our students' writing lives. Completing a worksheet on sentence fragments would be much less successful than teaching the importance of complete sentences in informational writing. Whatever your reason for including a minor, deciding on it clearly in the planning stage is important.

In our example, our major focus is the use of tools to aid writing. This is general enough to include all of the related standards and yet specific enough to enable us to pinpoint lessons. I decided on the minor focus (using the computer as a writing tool) because I feel it is important and because I am integrating writing and technology standards. This unit assumes that students have already had computer experience during the year and that they have already been through a genre unit of study on informational articles.

Because we now have identified the major and minor focuses for our unit, we can now give the unit a clever and descriptive name. My thinking in including the informational article in my title was that when the students are ready to begin creating, they'll need some structure as to what they will create. Informational articles will be a perfect lens through which to view the teaching points in this study.

IDENTIFY YOUR UNIT GOALS

Once you have made the big decisions about your unit of study, it's time to start pinpointing the specific academic goals you want your students to reach during the unit. Your unit goals will come from three different sources: your standards, you, and your students.

Standards-Based Unit Goals

Your first step is to extract from the standards the specific goals you will set for this unit. Since our first obligation is to our writing standards, we must start there to outline specific teaching points we wish to address in the unit. Your standards may already be written in terms of academic goals, in which case they are easily transferrable to your unit planner. If not, it helps to translate your standards into easily achievable outcomes you think your students can meet.

The standard "Quote or paraphrase information sources, citing them appropriately" became the following two teaching points: *Include information from other sources in writing* and *Cite quotes in writing*. The standard, "Demonstrate basic keyboarding skills and familiarity with computer terminology (e.g., cursor, software, memory, disk drive, hard drive)" became *Use the computer to write, edit, and publish an article*.

Teacher-Choice Unit Goals

The beauty of this type of planning is that there is room for you to infuse your own lessons into these units. Be creative here! This is where you can make these units your own so they really sparkle. This is where you will make them rise above the standards.

The less intricate your standards, the more chances you will have to supplement the units you teach. If you are teaching a genre unit on poetry, but your standards only mention four poetry goals, you can make your unit three weeks long and supplement every other day with poetry lessons you love to teach.

The teacher-preference goals are all included for different reasons. I think it is important for teachers to make the point that not everything we read on the Internet is true, so I've included that goal. I included the goals about using "experts in their field" because I have a student in my (hypothetical) class whose father is a weather man that I've been asking to come in and speak to the class. I've included the goal about using photographic illustrations because I know we will be on the Internet and the inevitable question always is, "CAN WE PRINT?"

These teacher-preference teaching points are just as important as the standards because they give you the opportunity to exercise your professional muscle to bring what you think your students need and want to the table. Adding teaching points that interest you helps you personalize your units of study and keep them current. Placing your signature on your units in this manner will push your practice beyond the standards.

Student-Choice Unit Goals

So far we have 14 academic goals for our unit. If we teach writing every day and we make this unit four weeks long, we'll still have plenty of time to follow the natural curiosity that comes during our immersion period. I can say with near certainty that during immersion, when students are considering, exploring, and making critical observations about the tools that exist in the writing world, they will wonder about something or make a connection to something that I cannot anticipate in the planning of the unit. It is crucial to leave open time to explore these connections when your students bring them to the group. You will honor your students' learning process this way, tailoring the unit goals toward their own thinking and processing of the information. This is another critical element of above-standard teaching.

ESTABLISH THE UNIT LENGTH

You'll also want to have some idea of the amount of time you intend to spend in the unit you are planning. Take a look back at your unit goals. How much time will you need to meet them? Will some be teachable in one day? Will others need a few days of focused instruction? How intense are the goals of this unit? Make sure you have enough time to meet your standards-based goals, to address your own teacher-choice goals, while still leaving time for the inevitable goals that will emerge from immersion.

Our sample unit will likely need at least four weeks. Notice I used the words "likely" and "at least" here. There is no precise method for determining exactly how much time we will need for this unit. Four weeks is my best professional guess. It is possible that once you start this unit, this four weeks will either grow or shrink depending upon your students, you, and the way things pan out once you start. By staying flexible, you will be more responsive to the needs of your students.

DETERMINE THE END PRODUCT

What do you want your students to produce during the last stage (commitment) of the unit? Will your students be expected to publish something? Will you simply have students add a sample sentence to a collection on a bulletin board? Or will they be asked to journal or discuss their ideas about how they might use the information learned in the unit to further their writing skills in the future? It is important to understand what you'd like for them to produce, so that you can keep your lessons moving toward this goal.

Ready, Set, Teach! Turning Plans Into Lessons

So now you have identified all of the key elements of your unit of study. The next step is to consider how you will deliver these lessons and in what order. What methods will you use to deliver the teaching points to your students? In planning specific lessons, it becomes important to remember the stages of the unit (immersion, identification, guided practice, commitment) and the structure of the day (focused instruction, independent practice, wrap up). However, the style you use to deliver these lessons, the creativity you tap into when bringing these lessons to life, and the natural humanness you employ when conveying these messages is totally up to you.

Our sample fourth-grade unit might look something like this:

Unit Name: <u>Writing Tools to Help Craft Informational Articles</u>   **Unit Length:** 4 weeks

Unit Type: Process   Genre   (Strategy)   Convention

Unit Major <u>Tools to Aid Writing</u>   **Unit Minor** <u>Computer as a Writing Tool</u>

DAY	FOCUSED INSTRUCTION	INDEPENDENT PRACTICE	WRAP UP
1 Immersion	Introduce unit, explaining that there are many tools that can help with writing. Have partners explore collection of writing tools (several examples in a labeled bin).	Independently, students will continue to explore the various kinds of writing tools in the classroom collection. Students will investigate these tools, noting their unique qualities and how they differ.	Hold general discussion about the tools. Ask students to talk about what they noticed, and how they think these tools might be of some help to them in their own writing.
2 Immersion	Students will again explore the collection of tools, becoming more familiar with them and taking special notice of the differences between the various tools.	Independently, students will continue to explore the various roles the writing tools might play in their writing.	same as above
3 Identification	Name the almanac, dictionary, thesaurus, and encyclopedia. Model the use of each while writing.	Have students write in any way they feel comfortable. Invite students to use one of the tools to help in some way. Use part of this time for students to tell a partner which tool they used and how.	Start a chart of the various tools and what they do (see example on page 133).
4 Identification	Name the remaining tools (newspaper, Internet, magazine, experts). Model the use of each while writing.	same as above	Complete the chart.
5 Guided Practice	Model using paraphrased information from the Internet or encyclopedia while writing an informational article. Warn of copyright laws.	Students will write informational articles (a familiar genre). Students will attempt to include paraphrased information from another source.	Ask a few students to share their writing, explaining their inclusion of supplemental information.
6 Guided Practice	Start with copyright discussion. Explain that there is a way to use an author's exact words if you follow the rules. Demonstrate citing.	Students will include at least one citation in their writing.	Ask students to share their citation with a partner. Partners should check for proper formatting of citation.
7 Guided Practice	Explain that many sources have easy devices to use to look something up. Explain tables of content, index, appendices, etc.	Ask students to work with a partner today and attempt to use an encyclopedia or almanac to look up something of interest.	Have a successful partnership share about how it went. Discuss how they might incorporate what they discovered in their writing.

continued

DAY	FOCUSED INSTRUCTION	INDEPENDENT PRACTICE	WRAP UP
8 Guided Practice	Review the differences between a dictionary and thesaurus. Begin a Venn diagram.	Students will edit current writing, checking spelling with a dictionary and changing a few words for better word choice using a thesaurus.	Discuss how the dictionary and thesaurus helped. Add additional information to the Venn diagram.
9 Guided Practice	Review definitions of encyclopedia and almanac. Tell anecdote about the "olden days" when we only had book encyclopedias. Discuss how online encyclopedias are an improvement over books in this case. (Up to date information, free, anyone can use.)	Put students in groups with one book of an encyclopedia. Have each group identify something of interest in the book. Bring class back together and look up each group's topic on an online encyclopedia, noting the additional information, photos, etc.	Have students think about and plan ways you might use the computer lab to help with their current articles.
10 Guided Practice	(In computer lab) Demonstrate the use of search engine (broad vs. specific searches). Discuss ways to spot reputable sites. Explain that much on Internet is not true. Demonstrate images search.	Students search for information they can use in their article.	Students print a page of information to bring back to class to paraphrase or quote in their article.
11 Guided Practice	Show the organization of newspapers and magazines. Explain that both include writing in different genres, and that we have to be careful to know the genre so we can decide if the information is true or not true.	Students explore newspapers and magazines with partners to explore the format and organization of them. Students will discuss the genre of the different articles they find.	Identify a few students to share their discoveries. What was probably true? What can't be used as true because we don't know for sure?
12 Guided Practice	Explain that experts have added to the information we find in writing tools. Experts are people who know a lot about one thing. Introduce Jessica's dad and have him explain about being a meteorologist (20 minutes).	With a partner, students create a scenario where they may need to use Jessica's dad as an expert while writing an article. (Additional writing time after.)	Students share their scenarios where they might need to consult a weatherman.
13 Guided Practice	Elicit the help of a student. Model interviewing techniques. (Specific questions about the main focus of your article, open-ended questions, etc.)	Students pretend to be writing an article about the lunchroom lines and practice interviewing a partner using the techniques. (Additional writing time after.)	Students discuss, in groups, the ways interviewing might help their writing in the future.

continued

DAY	FOCUSED INSTRUCTION	INDEPENDENT PRACTICE	WRAP UP
14 Guided Practice	(In computer lab) Demonstrate the use of spell-check.	Students will bring hand-written articles to the lab for word-processing. Students will spell-check their work. (Two parents in to help this day.)	Have students share the ways the spell-check helped their publishing.
15 Guided Practice	(In computer lab) Demonstrate embedding a photograph from the Internet into an article.	Students will continue publishing their articles. Students will embed at least one photograph into their article. (Two parents in to help this day.)	Have students share how they think embedding a photograph in their article made it a more interesting article.
Identification or Guided Practice	Reserved for Topic Resulting From Immersion		
Identification or Guided Practice	Reserved for Topic Resulting From Immersion		
Identification or Guided Practice	Reserved for Topic Resulting From Immersion		
19 Commitment	Celebrate articles! Add a title and byline. Read to a partner.	Students add titles and by-lines, read to partner, revise if needed.	Collect articles and think of a name for the magazine.
20 Commitment	Reflect on the learning that took place. Review the tools and how they can help writers, no matter what they happen to be writing.	Students think about how the tools might help them in future writing projects. Share with partners how they might use the tools again.	Invite students to read their pages of the class magazine.

In the actual unit of study, I've turned the goals into practical lessons. I have addressed the standards and I have included some of my own lessons. This unit also allows for student exploration and discovery of the tools for writing. Our imaginary fourth graders will also have the peace of mind of knowing that they are able to work at their own personal pace while writing. I have included my own flair by incorporating lesson delivery I feel would be exciting to these students, and by jazzing up the standards-based lessons in ways that match my teaching style. I've managed the flow of my lessons through the four stages of the unit, and I've included the daily format to keep the community structured and healthy. This unit of study does it all. It meets and exceeds standards in a way that empowers students and their teacher.

Common Concerns Laid to Rest

As I travel around the country, I hear occasional concern from teachers about planning this way. Most of the loopholes that teachers bring to my attention are just common misunderstandings about how this planning works. Let's take a minute to address these common concerns.

Writing Tool	How it Helps...
- almanac	- gives true facts about a topic
- dictionary	- tells you how to spell words, tells you what words mean
- thesaurus	- helps you make good word choices
- encyclopedia	- gives you true facts about a topic
- Internet	- gives you information about a topic that may be true or not
- newspapers	- tell current events
- magazines	- include different genres related to a topic
- people	- tell you about their experiences or what they know

Some charts can be left up even after the unit is over.

WHAT IF I HAVE A WRITING PROGRAM AT MY SCHOOL?

This is no problem at all! Your writing program can easily be incorporated into the lessons you teach in your unit. If you plan through units of study, your writing program can offer you the method by which to deliver the specific lessons inside the units. You'll likely find materials you can use for focused instruction lessons, suggestions for independent practice, and even ideas for the wrap-up sessions. Your writing program might also include direct-teaching lessons that could be suitable during the identification phase, exercises or materials that can be used during guided practice times, or thoughts on how to celebrate during the commitment phase.

Your writing program may even suggest specific units of study. This can be wonderful, but keep in mind that the units of study suggested by your writing program may not be based in any way on your state standards. Also, in many programs, the units of study are the same at various grade levels, clumping grades K–2 or grades 3–5 into one book. This is not ideal either, since we want to be sure our students are exposed to a continuum that broadens each year.

This is where you, the professional, need to look at your program with a critical eye. Make sure you are designing units that (1) meet your state standards, (2) build on the previous grade's standards, (3) provide your students with a comprehensive balance of the Complete 4 writing skills (process, genre, strategy, and conventions), and (4) give your students the inspiration they need to be independent, enthusiastic writers.

Lesson Name: *Building Writing Muscles*

Unit Name: *Stamina*

Unit Type: *Process*   **Grade Level(s):** *3–5*

Focused Instruction: *"My daughter, Morgan, recently joined a swim team. I was a bit surprised when I watched her practice. It seemed so tiring! They swam for a whole hour straight every single day! Morgan was so tired in those first weeks, but you know what happened when she went to her first swim meet? She won a blue ribbon for first place. I think she won because of how hard she worked to build up her swimming muscles in those practices. She just kept getting faster and stronger. Writers need muscles, too. When you first start writing, you might tire out quickly because you don't have what's called stamina. Stamina is what you build up over time when you practice every day. Let's think about the main character in the book* Love That Dog *by Sharon Creech. As we read Jack's notebook entries, we could tell that he really built up his writing muscles during the year. In his entry on September 13, he says he doesn't want to write, but at the end, on June 6, his notebook entry is long and strong and beautiful. Turn to your partner and discuss how you think Jack built his writing muscles over the year."*

Independent Practice: *While writing, students attempt to mimic some of Jack's behaviors.*

Wrap Up: *Chart some of the tactics students can use to increase their writing stamina.*

Notes: *Sharon Creech's book mentioned above is a quick read–aloud and very powerful. Read it one time through to appreciate the story, and then read it a second time with an eye on how Jack's writing habits change over the course of a school year.*

WHAT IF WE USE A TRAIT-BASED PROGRAM?

Great! Trait-Based Programs describe qualities of great writing, qualities which should be present in your students' writing pieces. The qualities of great writing should certainly be a part of your writing year. When one of your students produces a piece of writing, you would of course want it to contain such features as excellent word choice and proper organization, use of correct conventions and distinctive voice.

Where these programs may help to evaluate finished writing products, you can design your units to teach students to incorporate the traits into

Lesson Name: *Onomatopoeia*

Unit Name: *Poetry*

Unit Type: *Genre*   **Grade Level(s):** *K–2*

Focused Instruction: *"Today I'm going to teach you a really long, super-amazing, college-student word. Watch me write it. (Write "onomatopoeia" at the top of a sheet of chart paper.) Let me tell you a little secret. Some people told me once that kids your age have no business learning words this big. They thought words like this were too hard for you! I told them that they obviously didn't know my kids! Okay, this word means something really fun in poetry. You know how some words, when you say them, sound exactly like what they mean? Like, "POP!" or "ZOOM" or "drip, drop, drip, drop." I'm going to read a poem by Mary O'Neill called 'The Sound of Water.' Give me a thumbs up every time you hear a word that sounds like what it means." (Read book, then chart some examples of these types of words.)*

Independent Practice: *Students write poetry today, incorporating onomatopoetic words.*

Wrap Up: *Students write more onomatopoetic words on the chart.*

their writing. The traits of quality writing will naturally and necessarily show up in your units of study throughout the year. Organization will be taught during your genre units. (You have to know what type of text you are organizing in order to teach writers how to organize it!) Voice will show up in genre units (voice may be different in memoir and expository text) or in strategy units that guide your students toward developing their own style. Word choice can be addressed in a process unit (Writers Make Important Choices), a strategy unit (Revising Text to Improve Meaning), or a genre unit (Historical Fiction). Because knowledge of the conventions is one of the Complete 4 skills, you'll include whole units on conventions in your balanced and comprehensive year. The point here is that when students write well, these traits will be present in their final pieces of writing.

Units Make It Manageable

Teaching through units of study is empowering. As we discussed, our brains process information that is gathered into patterns much more successfully than it can process unrelated strings of information. What this means for us as teachers is that our planning makes much more sense when we are clustering our academic standards into a focused unit of study designed around common goals. Our units become the containers, and our standards are sorted into these containers in logical ways. Once our standards are sorted in this way, the teaching of them is far less haphazard and much more purposeful. Our planning *and* our teaching become much more pleasurable, and our writing curriculum begins to feel rich and full.

Chapter 6

Sample Units of Study

"Attention students, we are now on a rainy day recess!"
—School secretary over loudspeaker

"YEAH!!! We can do more writing now!!!!!!!"
—Second-grade class in Milpitas, CA

Seeing is believing. Most teachers will agree that the most powerful type of professional development is simply to watch a class in action. Watching lessons play out in an authentic manner helps teachers think, "Oh, well . . . I can do that!" Watching while even the most veteran of teachers struggles with the little boy who simply must have the top of his head planted firmly on the carpet or with the Mandarin-speaking girl who puts forth a valiant effort to understand or with the 47 interruptions that occur during the "Uninterrupted Instructional Time" helps us all remember that there's no such thing as an exact science when it comes to the teaching of children. Yet watching a talented teacher create abundant opportunities for love and learning helps us think we can do it too.

In this chapter, we will take a look inside some sample units of study. It is my hope that you will look at these units and realize that this type of teaching can be both thoughtfully planned and pleasurably relaxed. Although it is probable that you will have time to include entire units in your year that address learning outside of the standards once you analyze your standards and recognize a need for balance, for the purposes of this chapter, all of the units included here are first aligned to state standards. In keeping with the theme of this book, I've also included ample opportunities within the units for above-standard learning as well as for spontaneous inquiry during immersion. These examples are shaded. Where there is no shading, the lessons align to state standards.

Kindergarten Sample Unit

Unit Name: Storytelling   **Unit Length:** 3 weeks

Unit Type: Process   Genre   Strategy   Convention

Unit Major Elements of Story   **Unit Minor** Listening

DAY	FOCUSED INSTRUCTION	INDEPENDENT PRACTICE	WRAP UP
1 Immersion	Tell students a story. Talk about the storytelling you do in your own life. Ask, "Do you tell stories? When? To Whom? About what?"	Students tell a story to a partner. They then draw a picture to record the story they told that day. Students can add writing or label drawing.	Ask a few students to share their stories with class.
2 Immersion	Tell information about a story-teller in your life. Read *Wilfrid Gordon McDonald Partridge* by Mem Fox. "Anyone can be a storyteller, regardless of their size!"	"Can you tell a story to help a friend or a relative remember something important?" Talk/draw/sketch/write	Ask a few students to share stories with class.
3 Immersion	"When we tell stories, it is great to have an audience we trust and feel comfortable with. Today we will draw a character, an animal or a person to whom we would be comfortable telling stories." (Hang these up near where students will work during IP so they can look at them when practicing stories. The back of a chair works well.)	Students practice telling stories to their drawn "audiences."	Share your observations of the storytelling the students did to their "audience" today.
4 Immersion	Invite a guest storyteller into the class. (Principal, intern, etc.)	Students tell/draw/write their own stories.	Discuss the guest story-teller's story.

continued

DAY	FOCUSED INSTRUCTION	INDEPENDENT PRACTICE	WRAP UP
5 Identification	Create a class chart: When you tell a story, you need to . . . • tell names of people or animals • let listeners know where it is taking place • tell about things that happened • use a lively voice	Practice telling a story to a partner, using character names, the place of action (setting), and a lively voice.	"How did it go? Were you able to include those important things in your stories today?"

6
Guided Practice
	"Storytellers tell stories about things they wonder about, things they remember, and things they imagine."
	    Teacher should model telling a story.
	    Students each select what kind of story they will tell today.
		Students tell a story to a partner. They then draw a picture to record the story that was told that day. Students can add writing/label drawing.	"Who told a wonder story?" (share) "Who told a remember story?" (share) "Who told an imagine story?" (share)

7
Guided Practice
	"Storytellers tell stories about things they wonder about, remember, and imagine."
	    Teacher should model the second strategy. Students select the kind of story they want to tell.
	    Model use of alphabet chart to attach words to a story (labels on drawing).
		Students tell story to a partner. Draw/sketch/write.	"Who found the alphabet chart helpful today? Can you tell us about that?"

8 Guided Practice	Read aloud: *The Red Mitten* by Jan Brett (or any story you love that has strong story elements). Talk about how storytellers add on to stories. Jan Brett started with one idea and then added on every page. "How can you add on to yesterday's story?"	Students add on to yesterday's story by telling to a partner, and then adding words when possible.	"Think about when you were listening to a story today. How did the extra words help the story?"
9 Guided Practice	Read aloud: *Wemberly Worried* by Kevin Henkes. Note the problem/solution. Model telling a story with a problem/solution.	Students incorporate problem/solution into their own stories.	Ask one student to share a story with a clear problem/solution.

continued

DAY	FOCUSED INSTRUCTION	INDEPENDENT PRACTICE	WRAP UP
10 Guided Practice	Read aloud: *Leo the Late Bloomer* by Robert Kraus. Note problem/Solution. Reinforce if needed: use of alphabet chart when you want to add labels to a story.	Students draw/sketch/write stories that include problem/solution.	Choose a student with a clear problem/solution in a story. Share.
11 Guided Practice	"Partners are strong listeners when they are being told a story. How can you tell if you were a good listener?" Students think-turn-talk: How can you tell you are being a strong listener?	Students tell a story to a partner. Listeners then record their partner's story in a picture. Students can add labels or words.	"How did that feel? Were you a strong listener? How did being a strong listener affect your drawing?"
12 Guided Practice	"When people have really great stories to tell, they share them with others. Today you will pick one of your stories and start getting it ready to share." (Invite parents.)	Students select their favorite story and practice telling it or work on the sketch or words.	Remind all that the storytelling celebration is coming in three days!
13 Commitment	Chart the important elements for students to include in their stories (characters, setting, problem, solution).	Students continue to tell, sketch, or write, making sure to include the items from the checklist.	"I noticed _____ working really hard today, looking at the checklist to make sure his story is ready for the celebration."
14 Commitment	"Tomorrow is our storytelling celebration! Today will be your final practice. Remember how important it is to use a lively voice." (Demonstrate a story using a flat voice, then again with a lively voice.)	Students practice storytelling with lively voices.	Check in, making sure everyone feels "ready" for celebration.
15 Commitment	"Welcome to our storytelling celebration!"	Students share their stories in groups.	Give compliments, final comments.

Unshaded: Activity addresses a New York State Standard for Kindergarten
Shaded: Activity addresses a teaching point that is supplemental to the New York State Standards for Kindergarten

KINDERGARTEN SAMPLE UNIT ARTICULATION

Kindergartners participating in this rich unit will enjoy learning that is aligned to the very rigorous and thorough state standards. They will also benefit from the inclusion of several lessons that supplement these standards, which enables the teacher to focus on specific, practical skills that will make sense to five-year-olds.

For example, the New York state standards clearly say that students in the elementary years should "create their own stories, poems, and songs using the elements of the literature they have read and appropriate vocabulary" (New York State Learning Standards for

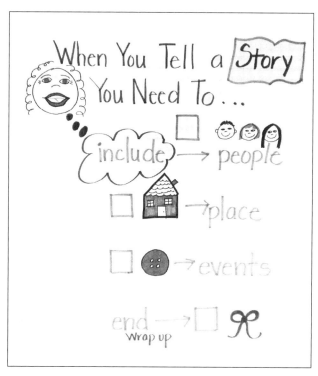

Icons help students understand expectations.

English Language Arts, Standard 2—Language for Literature Response and Reflection). This is a great jumping-off point, and the foundation on which this unit is built. But this unit develops this concept further by including lessons that define story elements such as character, setting, problem and solution—elements of story that kindergarten students can and should learn to incorporate into their own stories.

The state standards also clearly mention the art of listening in a set of standards called "Language for Social Interaction" (Standard 4). The unit minor (listening) is therefore chosen purposefully to align with this specific standard. This set of standards is designed to urge elementary age children to "listen attentively and recognize when it is appropriate for them to speak, to take turns speaking and respond to others' ideas in conversations on familiar topics, and to recognize the kind of interaction appropriate for different circumstances, such as story hour, group discussions, and one-on-one conversations" (New York State Learning Standards for English Language Arts, Standard 4—Language for Social Interaction). Many of the lessons in this unit support this, but since we are also leading our kindergarten students down the path toward representing stories in pictures and words as well as orally, we are pushing this specific set of standards just a bit further.

Our kindergarten unit includes specific lessons that gently direct the learning of our youngest students above the standard expectations of this age, but it also incorporates a teaching style that depends on query and inquest, which elevates our students to new heights beyond the standards. The teaching within this unit of study is more inclusive than what is specifically mentioned in the standards, and it makes use of highly active learning where our kindergartners participate in the process. We're not simply adding more to an already taxed calendar, but are instead teaching in a more comprehensive and empowering way.

Demonstrate the vast nature of nonfiction with this display before narrowing the study in your unit.

Grade 1 Sample Unit

Unit Name: Nonfiction Animal Reports   **Unit Length:** 4 weeks

Unit Type: Process   (Genre)   Strategy   Convention

Unit Major Report Writing   **Unit Minor** Organization

DAY	FOCUSED INSTRUCTION	INDEPENDENT PRACTICE	WRAP UP
1 Immersion	Introduce new unit, mark publishing date on the calendar. Give brief description of nonfiction text (true facts, to inform, etc.) Introduce anchor books collected into a bin labeled "nonfiction." Include nonfiction of all types in bin, but take care to include several animal books.	Students explore the books from the class collection, noticing the unique qualities of the various types of nonfiction.	Students share with a partner what they noticed about the various types of nonfiction. Distribute parent note asking students to bring in a sample of nonfiction text from home.

continued

DAY	FOCUSED INSTRUCTION	INDEPENDENT PRACTICE	WRAP UP
2 Immersion	Have students share pieces of nonfiction text brought in from home. What kind of nonfiction is it (e.g., recipe, directions, newspapers, etc.)? Express awe over how many different types there are.	Students continue to explore nonfiction texts from collection. Students begin to develop opinions about their favorite kinds of nonfiction text.	Students share their feelings about their favorite types of nonfiction. (Place examples of each type on a bulletin board entitled "Kinds of Nonfiction" and label each clearly—"newsletter," "animal books," "people books," etc.)
3 Immersion	Observe new bulletin board with class. "Wow, there sure are a lot of different kinds! I don't know about you, but my favorite by FAR is animal books! If I were writing a nonfiction book, I'd surely want it to be an animal book!" Take a vote: "Which kind of nonfiction would you like to write?" *(Disclaimer: If you don't think this will work, it is perfectly fine to just tell your class you are going to focus on animal books!)*	Once class has decided on animal books, students start to explore only animal books and notice what they can about this specific type of nonfiction text.	Students share what they are noticing. Chart observations.
4 Immersion	Having cleaned all other kinds of texts out of bin, select an animal book from the bin as an anchor text. Demonstrate "noticing" something about how the books are crafted. (e.g. "Hmmm . . . I noticed that animal books use real photographs").	Students explore animal books in groups, discussing the unique qualities of this genre.	Students share more observations, which are added to the chart.
5 Identification	"As a class, you made two important discoveries about nonfiction animal books. Some of you noticed that the books 'tell stuff' about the animal. We call these the 'true facts' in the books. Others of you noticed that the facts in the books are usually 'clumped together' sort of like chapters. We call this 'organizing' the facts into categories like 'what they eat' or 'where they live.' Today, read your animal books looking for these important parts of nonfiction animal books."	Students read, carefully noting these first two named elements of nonfiction—true facts and organized categories.	Students share examples of each of these elements they found.

continued

DAY	FOCUSED INSTRUCTION	INDEPENDENT PRACTICE	WRAP UP
6 Identification	"Another important discovery you made about nonfiction animal books is that the illustrations are different because they have writing on them. This writing is called 'labels' and 'captions,' and it helps demonstrate the true facts in the books. Today see if you can find books with labels and captions."	Students read, carefully noting examples of labels and captions.	Students share examples of labels and captions they found.
7 Guided Practice	Explain that when authors write nonfiction animal books, they do a lot of planning first to set up the book. Demonstrate using a graphic organizer such as a bubble web with an animal in the middle and categories of information around the outside.	Students select an animal for their report, and begin working on their bubble webs. Students will include at least four categories they wish to include in their books.	Share example of completed web with clear categories planned such as: *description*, *habitat*, *enemies*, *babies*, *food*, etc.
8 Guided Practice	Explain that another part of planning a nonfiction animal book is thinking about what true facts you might include in each section of information. Demonstrate talking through each section with a partner. ("I was thinking in the food section I should say that cats usually eat cat food but sometimes they eat mice and lizards too.")	Students will work with a partner to discuss ideas they can include in each section of their book.	Show an animal book completed by a former student in the expected format. Books can be as simple as a word or two on each page or as complex as an anchor text. It is important to validate all levels of production. Pass out blank books.
9 Guided Practice	Explain that authors of nonfiction usually include a lead that sparks the interest of the reader and makes him or her want to read more. Read a few examples of nonfiction leads from anchor books. Chart "Great Nonfiction Lead Ideas."	Students begin writing in their books. Students work on their leads.	Share a few examples of great leads written by students.

continued

DAY	FOCUSED INSTRUCTION	INDEPENDENT PRACTICE	WRAP UP
10 Guided Practice	"I was noticing yesterday as I was looking through these non-fiction animal books that they have incredible page design. That means that the authors took special care to make their pages look really, really interesting. The pages don't look like the pages in our stories. The words are all over the place, they have boxes of information, words in the illustrations, and detailed pictures."	Students continue working on their books with a focus on interesting page design.	Begin chart for interesting page design. Think aloud as you write. "Hmmm . . . maybe I'll write my words here. Then I can put my picture here, and I'll make it medium size so I can put a close-up picture here. I'll also leave room for when I want to write words in my picture. I'm going to color all the white space in my picture, too."
11 Guided Practice	"Remember when we talked about labels and captions? Today I'm going to explain about each of them." Use an anchor text to show that labels are simple words that point to things in a picture and captions are sentences that explain things more.	Students continue working on their books with a focus on adding labels and captions to their illustrations.	Add labels and captions to the chart started yesterday.
12 Guided Practice	Explain that sometimes authors of nonfiction text want to tell about something but they don't know the true fact yet, so they have to look somewhere else to find it out. This is called doing research. Demonstrate looking on the Internet to discover what a certain animal eats, for example.	Students continue working on their books, while rotating through computer stations to look up additional information on the Internet. (There are many variations of this that would work such as the computer lab, assigning this as homework, etc.)	Make an example of a student who wrote information from the Internet into his report.
13 Guided Practice	Explain that when we use true facts from another source like the Internet or a book, we have to make sure we don't copy it word for word. The information has to be said in our own words. Demonstrate paraphrasing from the Internet.	Student partners help each other make sure the researched information written into their books is paraphrased.	Use an anchor text. Model reading a true fact, thinking it is interesting enough to include in a report, and paraphrasing it before it is written.
14 Guided Practice	Explain that authors of nonfiction also tend to include a smart closing at the end. Show examples from anchor texts.	Students continue working on their books, focusing on a smart way to end them.	Have a few students share their closings with the class.

continued

DAY	FOCUSED INSTRUCTION	INDEPENDENT PRACTICE	WRAP UP
15 Guided Practice	Point out the differences between interesting titles like *Face to Face With Frogs* and plain titles like *Frogs*.	Students create interesting titles for their books.	"What interesting titles did you think of for your books?"
Identification or Guided Practice	Reserved for Additional Topic Resulting From Immersion		
Identification or Guided Practice	Reserved for Additional Topic Resulting From Immersion		
18 Commitment	"We are almost done with our unit and you are almost done with your books. You all need to make sure that you included the big ideas we talked about in this unit, so today we will make a list of all the things animal books should have." Make a checklist on chart paper of all expected elements (grouped information, good lead, detailed illustrations, captions and labels, closing, etc.).	Students continue working on their books, consulting the checklist to make sure they remembered to include all discussed elements.	"Did anyone use the checklist today and notice their book was missing something?"
19 Commitment	"Yesterday I noticed something really smart. I noticed _____ walking up to the checklist with a partner and his book to check to see if he missed anything in his book. Try this today."	Students continue working on their books, consulting the checklist to make sure they remembered to include all discussed elements.	Float around the room to enjoy the books.
20 Commitment	"Welcome to our publishing party!"	Students share their newly completed animal books with classmates.	Give compliments, general wrap up.

Unshaded: Activity addresses an Arizona State Standard for Grade 1

Shaded: Activity addresses a teaching point that is supplemental to the Arizona State Standards for Grade 1.

GRADE 1 SAMPLE UNIT ARTICULATION

First graders participating in this unit of study are set up for some incredible learning. Because of the way this unit is structured, first graders will feel as though they are simply "making something cool," which means they will be motivated to create projects to which they feel emotionally attached. The standard subject of nonfiction writing is whittled down to a comprehensible and interesting mode of nonfiction (animal reports) for our first graders. Students, having been asked to select their own subject matter for their books, enjoy active involvement in this unit which further empowers them, offering even the youngest of students some degree of choice in their learning.

The Arizona state standards do mention the expository genre for first grade in a brief two standards. First-grade students are expected to "create expository texts (e.g., labels, lists, observations, journals) through drawing and/or writing" and "participate in creating simple summaries from informational texts, graphs, tables, or maps" (Arizona State Writing Standards, Grade 1, strand 3, concept 2, PO 1-2). This unit meets these standards and it does so in a way that pushes expectations much higher and yet still remains reasonably age appropriate.

This unit challenges the degree to which first graders are held accountable to the skills in the standards. For example, where the state standards mention only that first graders must write a simple research report with a title and three facts, the first graders involved in this unit will be writing an entire animal book with "chapters" of organized information. They will be writing reports on topics in which they are interested and given ample time and structure to create more sophisticated texts. Even the lesson designed to create report titles is designed with a slant toward excellence. Why simply include a title, when first graders can tap into their imaginations and include an *interesting* title?

Standards other than the genre of nonfiction are met as well. The standards require that students will generate ideas through prewriting activities, and that students will organize ideas using simple webs. The organization and publishing lessons are designed to meet standards that address getting a piece ready for an intended audience. Finally, lessons are included to meet the standards

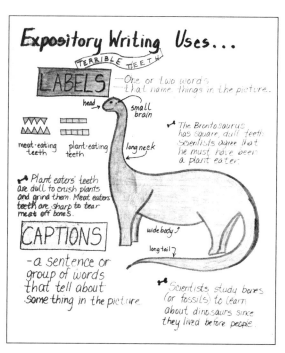

No subject is too small for a focused instruction lesson. Here, we discuss the use of labels and captions in nonfiction illustrations.

requiring students to write multiple sentences in an order that supports a main idea (Arizona State Writing Standards, Grade 1).

Like its kindergarten counterpart, the first-grade sample unit meets state standards, yet is much more comprehensive than the standards on which it is based. It seeks to elevate the first graders to a place beyond those standards. The first graders in this unit are expected to be inquisitive and independent. They are challenged to use their imaginations and to find their voices. The first graders in this unit of study are thinking, creating, and learning, and chances are they won't even be aware of the rigor of the lessons, because the learning in which they are actively engaged is relevant, purposeful, and embedded in a project designed by them.

Grade 2 Sample Unit

Unit Name: Letter Writing   **Unit Length:** 2 weeks

Unit Type: Process   (Genre)   Strategy   Convention

Unit Major Friendly Letters   **Unit Minor** Quotes/Caps Review

DAY	FOCUSED INSTRUCTION	INDEPENDENT PRACTICE	WRAP UP
1 Immersion	"People write letters for many reasons. Brainstorm reasons why people might write letters."	Students discuss reasons why they might write letters and to whom.	"To whom would you like to write a letter and why?"
2 Immersion	Pass out letter samples or put one on the Smartboard or projector. "As you can see, letters look a lot different from the text we'd see in a chapter book, newspaper article, or picture book. What do you notice about the way letters are written?"	Students continue to explore letters. Have samples or books with letters featured in them such as *Beethoven Lives Upstairs* by Barbara Nichol. Students notice what they can about letters.	"What have you noticed about the letters you've explored so far?"
3 Identification	"A lot of people write letters on e-mail these days. Unlike e-mails, when we write letters on paper, there are certain 'have-to's' about them. This is why they look like they do— because the writers know the rules of letter writing."	Students continue to explore letters with an eye toward the "rules." What do they think some of the "rules" of letter writing are?	"Did any of you notice anything you think might be a rule in letter writing?"

continued

DAY	FOCUSED INSTRUCTION	INDEPENDENT PRACTICE	WRAP UP
4 Guided Practice	Model writing a letter on chart paper. Think aloud about every "rule" as you follow it, such as putting the date in the upper right corner and a comma after the closing, etc. (Purposefully include a list sentence and a quotation in model letter.)	Students write letters, attempting to follow the formatting rules.	Begin checklist: "Important Features of Friendly Letters"
5 Guided Practice	In the model letter from day 4, underline the date, the salutation, the closing, and the signature. Explain proper placement for each of these.	Students continue to write letters, checking to make sure their date, greeting, closing, and signature are in the proper place.	Add "Date, salutation, closing and signature in the right places" to the features chart. Use model letter for review.
6 Guided Practice	Circle all the commas in the model letter from day 4. Explain that all the commas in the letter are included because there is a comma rule that says they go there. Review rules for commas in letters: greeting and closing, date, list sentences.	Students continue to write letters, carefully minding the placement of commas in their letters.	Add "Commas after the greeting and closing, in the date, and in list sentences" to the features checklist. "How did it go with the commas today?"
7 Guided Practice	Read aloud a boring letter and an exciting letter with tons of "voice" in it. You can write these yourself, or even make them up on the fly. Discuss the differences. Explain that when a letter has good voice, you can immediately tell who wrote it, because it comes alive and sounds like that person talking. Letters can be funny, sad, weird, whatever you want, but they should sound like you.	Students continue to write letters, attempting to employ voice.	Gather up some letters from a few willing students. Play "Guess Who?" Read the body of the letters, and see if the rest of the class can identify the writer. If they can, it probably has good voice.
8 Guided Practice	Continue voice topic. Make a T-chart with "No voice" and "Voice" at top. List flat sentences such as "It was a sunny day" next to voice-filled sentences such as, "It was so hot I thought my dog, Cali, was going to drink our whole pool!"	Students continue to write letters "just dripping with their voices."	Play "Guess Who?" again.

continued

DAY	FOCUSED INSTRUCTION	INDEPENDENT PRACTICE	WRAP UP
9 Guided Practice	Circle the quotation marks in the model letter from day 4. Review rule (previously taught).	Students continue to write letters. Students include at least one quote with proper quotation marks in their letters.	Add "Correct punctuation in the body of the letter" to the features chart. Ask two students with correctly used quotations to share their letters. Ask class to listen for the quotations.
10 Guided Practice	"In letters, we also have a lot of opportunities to practice our capitalization rules. Can you remember back to our capital rules and think of all the places the capitals should be? We are going to add two more today: the greeting and closing in letters." Highlight capitals on the model letter.	Students finish up with their letter writing by checking all capitalization within their texts.	Add "Capitals for dates, names, initials, greeting, closing, and the beginning of sentences" to features chart.
11 Guided Practice	Reserved for Additional Topic Resulting From Immersion	*Possible immersion outcomes to follow: letters as requests for change, letters of apology.*	
12 Guided Practice	Reserved for Additional Topic Resulting From Immersion	*Letters to express affection, attention-grabbing at the beginning of letters, questioning in letters, responding to letters with letters.*	
13 Guided Practice	Reserved for Additional Topic Resulting From Immersion		
14 Commitment	"What do people do with their letters once they are done? Check them against the features checklist and then SEND THEM!" Model address formatting on envelopes.	Students prepare their letters for sending by placing in envelopes and addressing the envelopes.	Students pass out letters to friends, deliver them around school, or place in backpacks for later delivery.
15 Commitment	Discuss how letter writing might be useful going forward.	Students make a list in their notebooks of future letters they may write.	Give compliments, general wrap up

Unshaded: Activity addresses a California State Standard for Grade 2
Shaded: Activity addresses a teaching point that is supplemental to the California State Standards for Grade 2

Lesson Name: *Secret Letter Assignment (End Celebration for Friendly Letter Unit)*

Unit Name: *Letter Writing*

Unit Type: *Genre*   **Grade Level(s):** *K–5*

Take time to plan this lesson ahead of time. Assign each of the students in your class the name of a classmate. Students are to keep their assigned person a secret until the day their letters are shared. Ask students to write a letter to their assigned person, making it special for the recipient by including compliments and good wishes for that person (this can also be assigned as homework). Have a "Secret Letter Share Party" where writers hand-deliver their letters to the recipients. (This is a nice lesson to plan for a winter holiday or Valentine party.)

GRADE 2 SAMPLE UNIT ARTICULATION

Second graders participating in this unit of study will certainly learn all about the nuts and bolts of writing a friendly letter, but these students will also receive hands-on experience with their newly acquired information in a way that feels authentic. Because of the way this unit is structured, second graders will embark upon a collective exploration of "this thing called letter writing." They will be encouraged to go find out about it, see what they can see, try it on for size. In the process, they will learn that they have to follow the rules while writing a letter, but that there is also a lot of wiggle room in letter writing for them to express their personalities. What better way to utilize voice than a personal letter?

The California state standards on which this unit is based outline the specific conventions of letter writing. "Write a friendly letter complete with the date, salutation, body, closing, and signature" (California ELA Standards, Writing, 2.2). From this, teachers can get a basic understanding of what they should teach with regard to letter writing. But why not spice it up a bit? Why not add voice? And why not use this unit as an opportunity to follow the interests of your children? From experience, I know that when given permission to do so, second graders absolutely love to add to the learning in their classrooms. They'll want to write letters to famous athletes (Why not?), to their parents (Sure!), and even to their dogs (Okay!).

This unit rises above the standards as well. Where the state standards mention only that second graders must write a letter including a few select elements, the second graders involved in this unit will be writing letters that employ sophisticated writing craft. Our students will be writing in a tone of voice that identifies them. They will be exploring themselves as writers, turning inward and asking, "What *do* I sound like when I talk, and how can I bring that into my writing?"

All this excitement aside, the most important element that boosts this unit up over the standards is time—time to explore and time to practice. Donald Graves reminds us that the very best way to teach children to write is to give them time to write (1983)! This unit of study builds in ample time for our second graders to practice their new knowledge, put it into play in real writing, try on a few things to see if they fit.

Grade 3 Sample Unit

Unit Name: <u>Editing for Clean Grammar</u>   **Unit Length:** 1 week

Unit Type: Process   Genre   (Strategy)   Convention

Unit Major <u>Editing</u>   **Unit Minor** <u>Grammar Review</u>

DAY	FOCUSED INSTRUCTION	INDEPENDENT PRACTICE	WRAP UP
1 Immersion	"See all these books we have around? The way they are made is really interesting. You might think that one person writes the book, but really there is a team of people who make a book. There is one person on the book-making team that is really important—the editor." Explain an editor's role.	Students explore books, looking for the names of editors in the books they read. Students discuss the "invisible partners" of their favorite authors. Students write down the name of an editor of their favorite author.	Make a chart entitled, "No Writer Works Alone." List favorite authors and their editors side by side, showing students that behind every great author is an editor.

continued

DAY	FOCUSED INSTRUCTION	INDEPENDENT PRACTICE	WRAP UP
2 Identification	Review the role of an editor. Explain that an editor helps by pointing out places where the author can make the writing better. Explain that editors use tools in their work, like a checklist. Mostly, an editor edits only after the writer has first checked the piece.	Explain that together you are going to make an editing checklist that can be used by student writers and student editors. (Make the tool, focusing on the following standards-based, previously taught conventions: subject and verb agree; pronouns agree; verb tenses match; spelling is correct; punctuation is correct; along with any other features of polished writing students feel are important.	Tell students that now that you have an editing tool, you are going to type it up so that tomorrow, you can use it for editing. For each item, include two check boxes, one for the author and one for the editor.
3 Guided Practice	Show students the newly typed and copied editing checklist based on the chart they developed yesterday. Model using it on your own writing, making check marks on the page when you have edited for each item.	Students work to reread a piece of their own writing, editing it with the new checklist, and making checkmarks when each item is correct or fixing a missing or incorrect item in the piece.	"How did it go today with the new checklist? How do you think editing helps our writing become better?"
4 Guided Practice	Tell the students that today they are going to play the role of the editor, which means they are going to edit someone else's work. As authors, the students are going to get help from an editor. Model editing someone else's writing.	Students partner up and edit each other's writing, making checks on the checklist and signing their names as the editors of those pieces.	Have a few students share how they did with the editing. "Did anyone's editor find something that you missed when you edited your own paper?"
5 Commitment	Discuss the importance of signing your name on an important document. Explain that signing our name is the same as saying, "This is all true, I promise." Explain that signing a checklist means that you are saying you checked everything and it is all there.	Students make final edits with partners. When students are comfortable with everything being correct, they sign their names to the checklists, staple the checklists to the pieces, and turn them in to the "copy editor" (you) for final review.	Give compliments and final comments. Explain that if there is any trouble in the copyediting department, the copy editor will call both the author and editor in for a private conference.

Unshaded: Activity addresses a Texas State Standard for Grade 3
Shaded: Activity addresses a teaching point that is supplemental to the Texas State Standards for Grade 3

GRADE 3 SAMPLE UNIT ARTICULATION

The bulk of this quick third-grade unit incorporates something over and above what is required by the state standards in the area of editing. Third-grade teachers are required to teach their students to "edit writing toward standard grammar and usage, including subject-verb agreement; pronoun agreement, including pronouns that agree in number; and appropriate verb tenses, including *to be*, in final drafts" (Texas Essential Knowledge and Skills, Third

Editing Checklist

- ☑ All "No Excuses" Words are Spelled Right.
- ☑ Every Sentence has a . ! or ?
- ☑ I followed the comma rules.
- ☑ I followed the apostrophe rules.
- ☑ I used quotation marks " " when people talk.
- ☑ I did a verb check (action words).
- ☑ My subjects and verbs agree.
- ☑ My word choice is outstanding.
- ☑ My sentences are interesting and different.
- ☑ I used some pronouns (he, we, us, etc...)
- ☑ Capitals are in the right places (first word, titles, proper nouns)
- ☑ My piece makes sense from beginning to end.

Is your writing CLEAN?

Checklists can be printed on paper as well so students can write on them.

Grade, 17(E). Third graders are also asked to "edit for appropriate grammar, spelling, punctuation and features of polished writing" in 18(D). Finally, third graders are required to "respond constructively to others' writing" in 19(B). This unit combines these relatively bulky standards into a one five-day unit.

This unit goes beyond the simple requirement of students editing for these conventions in several ways. First, in this unit, the student is not only asked to practice editing of her own piece of writing but also to experiment with editing another writer's piece. Third graders in this unit are also given the rather grown-up responsibility of applying their signatures to a contract. Finally, these third graders are introduced to the way in which the publishing industry works through such notions as the role of the editor, the idea of partnering with a "second set of eyes," and through the idea of a team approach to writing.

This unit is proof positive that by "above standard," I don't simply mean "more." This unit is only five days, and instead of simply adding more teaching points to our already strained calendar, the unit is broader and more heavily anchored to the real world of writing. This unit takes the suggested standards and reaches for a creative way to present them. In doing so, the unit is naturally stimulating without being excessive.

Grade 4 Sample Unit

Unit Name: <u>Writing Book Reviews</u>   **Unit Length:** 3 weeks

Unit Type: Process   (Genre)   Strategy   Convention

Unit Major <u>Responding to Literature</u>   **Unit Minor** <u>Citing Evidence</u>

DAY	FOCUSED INSTRUCTION	INDEPENDENT PRACTICE	WRAP UP
1 Immersion	Introduce book reviews. Read a few aloud. Explain that book reviews are in magazines, newspapers, and on the Internet.	Students explore various book reviews (gather a collection ahead of time). Students read reviews and start getting familiar with the genre.	"What are you noticing about book reviews so far?"
2 Immersion	Read two more book reviews to class. Ask students to start thinking of things all book reviews should have in them. Students turn and discuss with a partner.	Students continue to explore the class book review collection, continuing to think about the necessary elements of a review.	"What are you noticing about book reviews?"
3 Immersion	Tell students that you have noticed they have been making a lot of smart discoveries about book reviews so far. Chart the key elements of a book review (brief synopsis of the book without giving away the ending, characters, setting, conflict, theme, author's opinion, recommendation).	Students continue to explore the class book-review collection, thinking more now about the list just created. Students try to find those elements in their book reviews.	Choose a student who has identified a book review with most of the elements from the chart and ask him or her to share with the group.
4 Identification	Explain that when people write book reviews, they do follow a sort of template that includes all of the items on the list. They know the "rules" for review writing, and they generally follow them because book reviewers get paid to follow those rules. Book reviewers don't only write about books they like. You can usually tell by reading a review if a reviewer liked the book or not.	Students read book reviews in pairs. They discuss why it is important for the reviewers to follow a certain template. Students also discuss whether they feel the reviewer liked the book or not. Students select a book to review.	"Did anyone read a review that sounded like the writer really liked the book?" (Share) "Did anyone read a review that sounded like the writer really did not like the book?" (Share)

continued

DAY	FOCUSED INSTRUCTION	INDEPENDENT PRACTICE	WRAP UP
5 Guided Practice	"The first part of a book review usually tells what the book is about. This is called a *synopsis*. Book reviewers leave off the ending of the synopsis so they don't spoil the surprise." Students each look for the synopsis in a sample book review and share with a partner.	Students begin writing their book review by starting with the synopsis.	Students share their book and the synopsis in small groups. Students make sure their classmates didn't give away the ending in their synopses.
6 Guided Practice	Read a few examples that show how book reviews include characters and setting. Point out compact, vivid sentences.	Students add characters and setting to their book reviews.	Partners discuss vividness of sentences.
7 Guided Practice	Reiterate that writers of book reviews are careful not to ruin the surprise of the book. One way to make people want to read a book is to really emphasize the problem, but not mention the solution. Read a few examples.	Students continue to write their book reviews, adding the main conflict.	"Does anyone want to share their synopsis so far to see if the description of the problem really gets us to want to read the book?"
8 Guided Practice	Sometimes, if there is a strong life lesson in the book, the book reviewer will include that, too. Read examples of theme expressed succinctly in book reviews.	Students continue to write their book reviews, by telling the audience what they might learn from the book.	"Would anyone recommend their book to a teacher who really loves to read books with great life lessons? Why?"
9 Guided Practice	"Have you noticed that some of the book reviews are funny? Have you noticed that some seem angry?" Explain that the best book reviews use strong voice to express how the writer felt about the book. The writer is trying to make you feel the same way.	Students read book reviews with an eye toward whether they feel anything when they read them. Do they feel scared? Disappointed? Excited? Why?	"Did the book reviews you read today affect the way you feel? Did they make you feel a certain feeling about the book even though you may not have even read it yet?"
10 Guided Practice	"Book reviewers first read a book and then they figure out how they feel about that book. The last thing they do is write so that the words they choose match the way they feel about the book." Read a book review with an obvious feeling associated with it. Discuss.	Students go back to their book reviews or start new ones. Students try to identify how they feel about the book, and then get that feeling into their writing.	Choose a few students to read their book reviews. After each, listening students turn and discuss whether they felt the reviewer liked or didn't like the book.

continued

DAY	FOCUSED INSTRUCTION	INDEPENDENT PRACTICE	WRAP UP
11 Guided Practice	Review the concept of voice. Suggest that when you read a book review, you should be able to get a feeling for who wrote it. Read a sample from the class. Have students guess who might have written it.	Students continue to write book reviews, considering whether their classmates would be able to tell they were the ones who wrote it.	Collect a few class samples (with permission). Read aloud. Ask students to try to identify the writer.
12 Guided Practice	"How should we use book reviews? Should we trust them? Should we think they are absolutely, hands-down the truth, or are they just someone's opinion?"	Students begin to publish a book review by editing and revising or by rewriting a book review they will add to the class collection.	"Whose book review would you trust to be similar to your own opinion? Why?"
13 Guided Practice	Reserved for Additional Topic Resulting From Immersion.		
14 Commitment	Reserved for Additional Topic Resulting From Immersion		
15 Commitment	Review how book reviews are used in the world. "Why do we need them? Who reads them? How can you use them?"	Students collect their book reviews into a literary magazine. Name the magazine, bind it, and gift it to another class or to the school library.	Give final comments and compliments.

Unshaded: Activity addresses an Arizona State Standard for Grade 4
Shaded: Activity addresses a teaching point that is supplemental to the Arizona State Standards for Grade 4

GRADE 4 SAMPLE UNIT ARTICULATION

Again, this sample unit meets the state standards for responding to literature, and the elements the state has deemed necessary in this type of written response. And again, this unit rises well above these simple requirements to create an exciting experience for the students in this class. Instead of hearing about how to respond to literature (aren't there infinite ways to respond to literature?) these students are immersed in book reviews—real texts that exist in the literary world. These students are invited into a new world, and a new genre of text they may have never experienced prior to this teaching. They are shown that this type of text exists all around them—in magazines, newspapers, and on the Internet. The fourth graders will finish this unit with a clear understanding of why this type of text exists in the world, and knowledge about how they can best use book reviews going forward. The required lessons and supplementary lessons work side by side in the spirit of exploration and discovery to create a unit that rises well above the standards.

Grade 5 Sample Unit

Unit Name: Crafting the Literary Essay   **Unit Length:** 4 weeks

Unit Type: Process   (Genre)   Strategy   Convention

Unit Major Literary Essay   **Unit Minor** Organization

DAY	FOCUSED INSTRUCTION	INDEPENDENT PRACTICE	WRAP UP
1 Immersion	Post the questions: "What is a literary essay?" and "What is literary criticism?" on a chart or wall. Explain that these two questions will be the focus of the next two days. Introduce your collection of literary essays. (Find editorial reviews of similar books on www.amazon.com.)	Students read literary essays, becoming familiar with the genre. Students discuss what they are starting to notice. (Give students controlled time for both reading and discussion.)	Begin discussion about the answers to the two focus questions. Infuse the discussion with information about the genre, bringing the class to a collective definition of the genre.
2 Immersion	Explain that literary essays have certain specific elements and that literary essays serve an important purpose in the literary world. Write two new focus questions: "What are the elements of a literary essay?" and "What is the purpose of a literary essay?"	Students read literary essays with an eye on the focus questions for the day. Students discuss what they are noticing about the specific elements and purpose of literary essay.	Facilitate whole-class discussion, adding elements of a literary essay to the chart. End discussion with a collective definition of the purpose of a literary essay. "So I guess we all agree that a literary essay is a writer's opinion about a piece of writing, including examples to prove his point."
3 Identification	Discuss how a literary essay is a writer's opinion or point of view about a piece of writing. Read the beginning of a sample essay, calling attention to the writer's thesis statement.	Students read literary essays in pairs, discussing and highlighting the writer's thesis statement.	Partners share their discoveries with the whole class.

continued

DAY	FOCUSED INSTRUCTION	INDEPENDENT PRACTICE	WRAP UP
4 Identification	Identify the place in the introduction where you find the writer's thesis statement. Explain that this is where the reader is told what the writer's position or opinion is and how the ideas in the essay will be arranged. Read "The Road Not Taken" by Robert Frost (or any other strongly themed poem).	Students discuss the shared poem in pairs, practicing writing a thesis statement for a literary essay.	Students share their practice thesis (opinion) statements with the class.
5 Identification	Repeat yesterday's lesson with a different poem.	Students discuss the shared poem in pairs again, practicing writing a thesis statement for a literary essay.	Students share their practice thesis (opinion) statements with the class.
6 identification	Explain that after the thesis statement that details the writer's opinion, the next element of the literary essay is the body of the essay. In the body, the writer offers examples from the piece of literature to prove her point.	Picking up from the day before, students work with the same partners as they identify three examples from the poem that prove their thesis statement.	Discuss some of the examples found and how they serve to prove the various thesis statements.
7 Identification	To follow an easy structure, suggest that the body include three paragraphs. Each paragraph is written around one example, or piece of evidence from the piece of literature. Read sample essay to demonstrate.	Student partners write the three "proof" paragraphs that correspond to their examples found yesterday.	Share some examples of paragraphs.
8 Identification	Explain that literary essays have conclusions. Read another example of a literary essay. Focus on the concluding paragraph.	Students read literary essays, identify the conclusions, and discuss a possible conclusion for their practice essays.	Discuss the purpose and importance of the conclusion.
9 Identification	Explain that in the next phase, students will be writing their own literary essays. "Writers of literary essays choose to write about pieces of literature that 'speak' to them in some way. When writers feel something for the piece they are writing about, the crafting of the essay feels easier."	Students search poetry collections and identify a poem they will use for their own literary essay. Students will select a poem which evokes in them some emotion or strong opinion.	Students share their poem with a partner and explain why they chose that poem.

continued

DAY	FOCUSED INSTRUCTION	INDEPENDENT PRACTICE	WRAP UP
10 Guided Practice	Review the thesis statement. Explain that students will first need to identify what they will be saying in their essay. What is the purpose of their essay? What exactly will they be attempting to prove to the reader about this piece of literature?	Students formulate their thesis statements.	Students read their thesis statements to a partner. Partners discuss the strengths of the thesis statements.
11 Guided Practice	Explain that once the writer has formulated a thesis statement for the literary essay, he can plan the rest of the essay. Model how to extract three examples from the piece of literature and to plan the three-paragraph body of the essay.	Students identify three examples from the text of their poems, which they will use for their three paragraphs.	Students share their examples with a partner, articulating why these examples will prove their thesis statement.
12 Guided Practice	Explain that writing can begin when planning is complete. Talk about craft. Explain that the best essays, the most exciting ones to read, have excellent word choice, voice, and so on. Explore samples for great leads.	Students begin to write their literary essays, carefully crafting an excellent lead.	Choose a few students to share their excellent leads with the class. Discuss how these leads are exciting and make the reader want more. Also discuss how sometimes writers will write several leads, revising and choosing a favorite.
13 Guided Practice	Teach the proper way to cite examples from the piece of literature by reviewing the use of quotation marks for exact text used in the essay. Model.	Students continue to write their literary essays with an eye toward the correct format for quoting text.	Ask students to check their cited examples for proper format. (Partners can also check each other's.)
14 Guided Practice	Explore the use of vivid and descriptive word choice in literary essays. Read examples, pointing out why they are strong.	Students continue to write their literary essays with an eye toward vivid and descriptive word choice.	Students read excerpts from their essays to partners. Partners close eyes and determine whether the words "paint a mind picture."
15 Guided Practice	Discuss transitions from one paragraph to the next. Explain how transitions make the writing flow smoothly from one idea to the next. Chart some ideas for smooth transitions.	Students continue to write, with an eye toward transitions.	Students do quick checks of each other's work for smooth transitions.

continued

DAY	FOCUSED INSTRUCTION	INDEPENDENT PRACTICE	WRAP UP
16 Guided Practice	Explain the importance of a conclusion. Explore examples.	Students continue to write, focusing on a strong concluding paragraph.	Select a few students to share strong conclusions.
17	Reserved for Additional Topic Resulting From Immersion.	Students continue to write, revise, edit, and publish their literary essays.	
18	Reserved for Additional Topic Resulting From Immersion.	Students continue to write, revise, edit, and publish their literary essays.	
19 Commitment	Review what has been learned about literary essays, and how this will help students going forward. (Explain that this type of writing will be expected in the upcoming years of school.)	Students continue to polish their literary essays.	Select a few students to read their completed literary essays to the class.
20 Commitment	Publishing party!	Students share their literary essays with guests.	Give final comments and compliments.

Unshaded: Activity addresses a New York State Standard for Grade 5
Shaded: Activity addresses a teaching point that is supplemental to the New York State Standards for Grade 5

GRADE 5 SAMPLE UNIT ARTICULATION

This is a nice example of a unit of study that addresses several state standards at once. This unit does a brilliant job of drawing together several standards under a large subject of study. This unit successfully anchors what could have been unrelated, individual skills to a sensible project on which fifth graders can easily focus. The fifth graders in this four-week study are engaged in the rather advanced genre of literary essay, practicing such needed writing strategies as planning, editing, revising and publishing, and trying on such complex behaviors as literary discussion and partnerships.

Almost all of the lessons in this unit of study are standards-aligned, leaving what may seem like little room for more. However, to the keen eye, it is apparent that these fifth graders are enjoying a breadth of learning that in fact does extend beyond the key standards skills that are overtly addressed. This unit of study places the students in an active role. Our fifth graders are not simply being presented with definitions of literary essay, the proper way to plan, or the correct way to cite a quotation. Instead, these fifth graders are exploring these standards-based skills cohesively, in a real way—a way that enables them to discover these skills (and more) on their own. Because the lessons are rooted in a real class endeavor, a real kind of writing, and because the lessons here are part of a greater whole, these students will indeed challenge the very standards on which this unit is based.

You'll note that this unit also allows for a couple of days during which the teacher may address the natural curiosities of the students surrounding this type of learning. Perhaps one student has a relative who is a literary critic. Perhaps a student will discover that the articles in her favorite magazine that she had been enjoying for so long are in fact literary essays by definition. Or perhaps another student, who is typically the last to make a decision during library visits will realize that literary essays can help take the edge off the selection process. Wherever these students lead, the teacher in this fifth-grade class will have the room to follow.

It's All About the Kids

As I hope these units have helped you see, teaching above standard is not at all the same as austere, rigorous teaching that merely exposes children to subject matter beyond their grade levels. These units are chock full of learning that goes beyond the average expectations, but they do so because the learning revolves around the students. It's not that the units include more "things," it's that the units explore the teaching points more broadly. It's not that the students of these lessons are working harder, they are working smarter. It's not that teachers are expecting excellence, it's that they are expecting activity. It's not that these kids are being forced to perform, they are being challenged to think, and they are enjoying themselves in the process.

Chapter 7

Assessment

"No man is good enough to govern another man without that other's consent."
—Abraham Lincoln

Ah, conference time! The image always strikes me as funny—adults hunched over little tables shaped like rainbows, wedged into teensy chairs while attempting to hold very serious conversations under charts that say "Remember the Golden Rule" or "Save the Drama for Your Mamma." Call me crazy, but I always looked forward to parent-teacher conferences. I thought it was nice, even just a few times a year, to chat about my professional efforts with someone older than six. Sure, students show us their affection in many different ways (the "I love you sooooooooo much" note from a first grader or the "I guess you're-kinda-cool-after-all" knuckle bump from a fifth grader). However, it is rewarding in a different kind of way to have our students' parents give us an approving nod. We share a common affection with these adults—the special little people with whom we spend our days—and that automatically makes us partners.

I find I have a lot to say during conference time, which means I usually run a bit behind. Most parents give me a break, thank goodness, and attribute this to how well I get to know their children! I have a lot to talk about because I feel it is important to address two types of information—the informal data I gather while interacting with my students and the more formal assessment data I collect from them.

Naturally, I think the informal observations are much more interesting, as do the parents. I know what my students' current interests are (Bobby is a crack skateboarder who is saving every penny to buy new wheels for his board). I know what is going on in their families (Beatrice had twin baby sisters born at the beginning of January. Stephen's dad broke his ankle playing Frisbee the other day). I know the patterns of how my students prefer to work (Kendra holds her pencil in a way I've never seen and Nal has to be sitting on his chair backward to get anything done). I know how they best learn (Malik has a hard time processing what I say until the message travels via music, and then he never forgets. Yasmin constantly battles for total silence around her). I figure I can best teach my students (and enjoy going to school with them every day) when I know them as the interesting people they are. We are all going to hang out together for six and a half hours every day for an entire school year, so we may as well get to know, appreciate, and support each other!

I also feel I should share the formal data I have for each child during conferences. Some parents really want the numbers. I have the data, so why not share it? I have data from formal tests and from unit assessments I've designed. These help me reflect on my students' achievements as well as on my own teaching.

As a teacher of above-standard writing, you'll want to give some thought to collecting both types of data—informal, observational assessment data as well as formal assessment data. Much of this teaching is individualized, so

FROM THE PLAN BOOK

Lesson Name: *Family Trees*

Grade Level(s): *K–5*

A wonderful way to support your student writers is to send home a family-tree project. My grade-level team did this every year, and we enjoyed the elaborate, colorful trees that came in nicely decorated with family pictures, flags, and adornments. We learned about our students' families and home lives, but more importantly, our student writers learned more about themselves. While making their trees at home with their parents, our students heard family stories, learned about their family heritage, met new members of the family through pictures and remembered fond family memories. Inevitably, the work they put into their trees wove its way into the writing our students did in class, particularly during our narrative writing unit. Also, when we found our writers suffering from writer's block, we could take them over to their family tree to jog some memories.

the more you know about the particular skills of each of your writers, the more you will be able to continue to push them toward where they need to go. Your formal data will help you reflect on the success of your instruction. Do your students generally understand the teaching points you are delivering? Are there teaching points that you need to revisit? Where will you go next? The formal assessment data you gather can help you answer these questions and more. Plus, you'll have a lot to talk about at conference time!

Teacher Observation

You already do this every day of your life as a teacher. Observing your students and their glorious idiosyncrasies certainly provides excellent entertainment. But if you focus on the writing behaviors your students are exhibiting during writing time each day, you can really gain quite a lot of information—information you can later use to propel students far above standard where appropriate, to reteach students where necessary, and to adjust your own teaching when needed.

This idea may be above standard in itself. In our current political climate, all the focus and attention is on the formal assessment data, but as professional educators, we know that the data we gather by observing our students is much, much more powerful in terms of truly identifying what we must do in order to get our students to acquire a skill.

CONFERRING

One way to gather observational data during your writing period is to hold conferences with your writers. Conferring is a complex activity with many nuances that can take a lot of practice to master. The writing conferences you have with your student writers should take place daily, with at least one weekly conference per student. Typically held during the independent practice portion of the day, conferences enable you to assess and to address writers' individual strengths and areas of need. Writing conferences are more than simple, informal discussions you hold with your students. Learning to exercise some discipline during this precious time will maximize the amount of data-gathering and teaching you can do within your conferences, a significant concern considering conferences are often limited to a mere five to ten minutes.

One of the conferences, though brief, offers mountains of assessment information.

For many teachers, conferring may be an intimidating proposition. You might fear not being able to get to all of your students. You might worry about not knowing what to talk about or what teaching point to focus on once you're sitting there with a student. I can assure you that though the routine may start off a bit uncomfortably for you at first, these conversations will eventually evolve into natural, friendly conversations (that just happen to follow a specific structure). Conferences feel more routine and more effective the more you engage in them.

Conferring is also one of the most important parts of writing instruction and is essential to the assessment process. By taking clear observational notes during these conferences, and by regularly reviewing your notes, you will easily identify the patterns of writing behavior that are happening within your class in direct response to your writing program. For example, when you notice that the entire class seems to be lacking a skill you already covered, you can adjust by reteaching that skill to the whole class in a focused instruction lesson. Similarly, when you notice that one or two students are struggling with a specific strategy, you can address that strategy in a subsequent conference. The data you collect during conferences will guide your practice by illuminating the opportunities you will have to go further with your teaching.

Your students will also become accustomed to talking about writing, so accustomed that they will feel safe enough to share the type of information that will be invaluable to you as a teacher of writing. You'll begin to know your students' interests (potential writing topics), fears (useful in breaking down barriers to the writing process), and strengths (upon which you will build more advanced learning). By building such a comfortable rapport with your students and validating the voices of those writers, you'll boost your teaching way beyond average.

Lesson Name: *Writing Goal Sheet*

Unit Name: *Launching the Writing Period*

Unit Type: *Process*   **Grade Level(s):** *K–5*

Focused Instruction: *"We have talked about conferring, about how that is going to work, and that when we talk during a conference, I might give you a goal—something for you to work on until the next conference with me. (Holding up the Writing Goal Sheet). This is called your Writing Goal Sheet (Appendix page 201). You will keep it in your folder all year. I will write the goal I want you to work on until your next conference, so that we both remember it. Then, next time we meet, we'll look at the goal you were working on and decide if you've met it yet. If it seems that you've reached that goal, we'll give you a check mark and set a new one."*

Independent Practice: *Students put their blank goal sheets in their writing folders and wait for the next time they are called for a conference to use them.*

Wrap Up: *Discuss the importance of starting each day with a peek at your goal sheet.*

Finally, the validation a writer gets from just a few minutes of discussion about his or her efforts make conferring an indispensible part of teaching. Put simply, conferring builds confidence. If you start every conference by pointing out something spectacular that student has done in her writing, your students will come to believe they are spectacular writers. It is much easier to deliver a piece of constructive criticism after first celebrating how incredibly smart a writer is for having done a particular thing. I've seen even the meekest, most doubtful of students absolutely swell with pride during a writing conference. This is what we want for every one of our writers—total confidence and openness to suggestions for improvement.

Tips for Successful Informal Assessment and Teaching During Writing Conferences

It's ironic that it takes so much structured practice in order to make your conferences look, feel, and sound like normal conversations. Your ultimate goal is definitely a relaxed exchange, but you also want this exchange to be very full, which is the part that takes planning and consideration. In order to make your conferences as rewarding as possible for both you and your students, consider your roles before, during, and after the conference session.

Before the Conference

A little preparation can help keep your conferences on track. You should have some idea of what you'd like to cover with your students based on previous interactions. Go through your notes from earlier conferences and decide where you'll go with the next one. Have clarity about your student's strengths and areas for improvement before you meet with her. Set a goal for the conference and stick with it.

During the Conference

Always start off with a positive. Let your student know something that he is doing really well, and be genuine in your praise. "I noticed that you have been putting a lot of effort into the pacing of your story. I love how you used these words here: 'I felt like the world was under water that whole year.' That's really a powerful statement." Pinpointing a specific area to praise helps your student feel competent, so that when you get to the teaching point, he'll be more open to the constructive criticism you offer.

Ask open-ended questions throughout the conversation to gather more data as you proceed. Students will come to expect these types of questions and will grow more comfortable offering detailed answers. Carl Anderson's famous conference question, "How's it going?" demonstrates the type of expected articulation we have of our students in a writing conference (2000).

Open-Ended Discussion Starters for Writing Conferences

Tell me more about . . .
How is it going for you?
Explain to me why you . . .
How can I help you more?
What have you struggled with?
How are you feeling about . . . ?
Tell me your thinking about . . .
What did you mean by . . . ?
What would happen if . . . ?
Why did you . . . ?
How did you get the idea for . . . ?
Where did the idea for . . . come from?
Tell me about this part here.

Make your one teaching point for the conference clear to your student, and teach this new information in a lively and active way. Bring literature in where appropriate, using anchor books as examples of how authors have addressed a particular skill. "I think your writing may improve even more if you give some thought to crafting strong sentences with interesting structures. Let's take a look at the anchor texts together and see how other authors incorporated interesting sentences into their writing. Maybe you'll get some ideas that way." Close your conference with another nod to the teaching point, establishing the expectation that this writer will leave the conference to go work on implementing the new skill. (Recording the new learning on a Writing Goal Sheet will help you both stay on track.)

After the Conference—Keeping Records

Give some thought to how you will want to collect your observational data ahead of time. How to take notes is an individual decision every teacher must make. What works for one person may not work for another, so you have to come up with a system that works best for you. Teachers are so vastly different in how they organize and process information. This is one area where you really have to decide for yourself what will feel most useful.

SUGGESTIONS FOR NOTE-TAKING DURING OBSERVATIONAL ASSESSMENT TIMES		
Make a writing binder for yourself. Include a section for each student. Record observations in each student's section.	Carry a clipboard loaded with white label stickers. Record notes on stickers, then place in binder or files later.	Carry calendar printouts. Record observations in the date squares.
Create a folder or file for each student with blank pages inside. Record observations on blank pages.	Record observations on sticky notes. Place sticky notes in binder or files later.	Create a weekly log sheet with a section for each student. Record observations for each student. At the end of the week, it should be full.

Different Types of Conferences

Conferences don't always have to include you, the teacher, and one student sitting at a table. You can vary your conferences by meeting with two or more students at once, or by making allowances for other creative meeting ideas. You can dramatically affect the amount of assessment data you gather, the number of students you meet with on a weekly basis, and the amount of teaching you do within your conferences by carefully selecting the best format for your conferences.

Individual Conferences

Meeting one on one is one of the most powerful types of conferences you can have. Even if it's only for a few moments, your student has you all to herself to discuss the progress she is making in writing and to receive a lesson specifically designed with her in mind. During a one-on-one conference, you can also gather the most data about a single student because you have the undivided attention of that student with no interruptions.

FROM THE PLAN BOOK

Lesson Name: *The Off-Limits Symbol*

Unit Name: *Launching the Writing Period*

Unit Type: *Process*   **Grade Level(s):** *K-5*

Focused Instruction: *"Look at this beautiful necklace, everyone! It is beaded and colorful and lovely, isn't it? It is also very powerful during writing time. I wear it when I am busy with conferences and I need to give my full attention to the person I am meeting with. When I am wearing this necklace, it means that I'm 'off limits' for questions just then. Let's practice." (Role-play by having a student try to ask you a question and respectfully "tune out" the student's attempt while the necklace is on.)*

Independent Practice: *Students work independently. Put the necklace on and take it off several times during this period so that students can practice the rules of the necklace.*

Wrap Up: *"There might be a time when there is an emergency and I'm wearing the necklace. Let's think of what you might do if you have to go to the bathroom or have a real emergency." (I used a hand signal in my room, but anything goes.)*

Small-Group Conferences

You may also consider the small-group conference, during which you would address a few students with similar writing needs. As you review your conference notes, you may notice that two or three students are struggling with a particular aspect of writing. Instead of meeting with these students one at a time, simply pull all three of them into a conference together. Small-group conferences are also a way to differentiate for your gifted students. Pull them into a small-group conference and present additional teaching points to this group that you may not have necessarily addressed with the whole group.

The "Whack-a-Mole Conference"—A Special Nod to Teachers of Our Youngest Writers

Kindergarten teachers and even some first-grade teachers may have a more difficult time meeting with students in a structured one-on-one setting while the rest of the class remains independent. Successfully launching the routines of the writing period at the beginning of the year through a process unit that addresses expected behaviors during work time will help, but kindergartners are still quite young and needy at times. Working with a whole classroom of five-year-olds can at times feel like the Whack-a-Mole game at the boardwalk. Just when you've redirected one, another is popping up with a request.

The Whack-a-Mole conference style allows you to be on the move in the classroom. (And for you literal folks out there, no, you of course NEVER whack the children!) This type of conferencing (also known as "bent knee conferencing") enables you to walk around the room helping as many students as you can. This way, your students still feel your presence and attention in the room. You can bend down to a student, address a quick teaching point with her and move on. Note-taking is challenging with this style of conferring because you will be moving so quickly, but it remains a necessary part of your data gathering.

This presence in the room during writing time (as opposed to focusing on one or two students at the conference table) also enables you to keep an eye on your group so that you can refocus behaviors when they veer off task. Always do this in a positive way. Here is an example:

TEACHER: Everyone, I can see that you are all working very hard, but would you mind if I call a quick time-out for a minute?

(Students direct their attention toward the teacher.)

TEACHER: I noticed that Caleb is snuggled into his little writing nook over there, concentrating so hard on his writing today. He is doing such a great job working on his narrative story. I just wanted to take a minute and celebrate that because that is exactly what excellent writers do. They use their writing time to really work hard and focus on making their writing the best it can be. So we can all learn from Caleb today. Let's all make sure we are really on task and working hard during writing time. Okay, thank you. Time in.

For teachers of our youngest students, it is important to understand that conferring in any classroom can take time and lots of practice, and when you are teaching such young and eager students, conferring may be even more challenging. Give yourself the gift of figuring out a conferring style that feels comfortable and manageable. Work toward the formal conferences, but take the pressure off getting there right away. Make sure you are gathering the observational assessment data you need, know your students as writers, and do this in a way that feels right to you and to your students.

Formal Assessments

Formal assessments are also a critical part of bringing your student writing above standard expectations. Formal writing assessments can prove that your instruction is working to create empowered writers in command of their craft. They can also inform the direction you take in your teaching. You have a few opportunities to formally assess your students, including standardized tests and teacher-created unit-based assessment tools.

STANDARDIZED TESTS

These days, most teachers are responsible in some way for helping students succeed on standardized tests. Writing is usually one of the components of these tests. Even the SAT is no longer the 1600-point reading and math exam it once was. Today, the SAT is a 2400-point extravaganza, which assesses three subject areas: reading, math, and—you guessed it—writing. For our students, the stakes are higher than ever. Standardized tests will be in our students' lives throughout their academic careers, and no matter how we feel about the tests themselves, I'm sure everyone will agree that our students deserve the chance to ace them.

Preparing Our Students for Writing Tests

Because the standardized tests are typically state-designed, they are almost always aligned to your state standards, so the first thing you can do to ensure your students are successful is to teach with a keen eye on your standards. A good writer should perform successfully having been taught with an eye toward the grade-level writing standards, since that is what is tested. Even more powerful, when you take your writing teaching to a new level where you are teaching these standards (and more) in a way that turns your students into active, critical writers, they will ace these tests.

Many of these exams are created fairly (if the state standards on which they are based are clearly communicated) to assess specific qualities of successful writing. Exams typically look to assess the values outlined by the standards, but if your students have received a complete writing program that has addressed all four major skill areas of masterful writing, they have an even better chance of excelling. An exam might seek to measure whether a student can choose an appropriate genre of text to communicate to a specific audience (genre), whether a student can successfully make plans and set goals for writing (process), whether a student can employ individual voice in a piece of writing (strategy), or whether a student has command of proper punctuation (conventions). These requirements are quite fair if they are indeed based on the state standards. However, these skills are much too lofty to be panic-taught in just a few weeks before the test. Writing assessments treat writing as a major school subject, and therefore, our students deserve a focused writing curriculum that extends across all grade levels.

By teaching in the manner described in this book, you will give your students a leg up on their standardized assessments. Everything described in this book helps develop successful writers. With a yearlong commitment to above-standard writing, and with a structured yet flexible framework for writing that continues consistently all year long (and preferably across all years of a child's educational career), you will cultivate in your students the writing processes, genres, strategies, and conventions that excellent writers possess. When excellent writers attack these tests, they do well on them.

Lesson Name: *What Genre Are They Asking Me to Write?*

Unit Name: *Prompt-Writing*

Unit Type: *Genre* **Grade Level(s):** *3–5*

Focused Instruction: *"We have been getting you ready to put all of your amazing writing talents to work when you take your writing test. One of the first things you have to do when you read these writing prompts is ask the most important question of writing-test taking. The question is 'What genre are they asking me to write?' You have to search the question for clues. Let me read a sample writing prompt aloud and see if you can hear some clues about what the prompt is asking." (Read a sample and guide students toward language tip-offs such as "write a story," "tell about something that happened," "convince," or "persuade.")*

Independent Practice: *Students read sample questions with small groups and highlight trigger language that can indicate the genre they are expected to write.*

Wrap Up: *Small groups share their thoughts with the class.*

Writing Exam as a Unit of Study

Your entire year should be designed to prepare your students for their writing exams. Still, you can also add a unit of study that focuses on writing-test taking that may help your students best prepare for what they will encounter. All writers can benefit from looking at these prompt-based tests as a unique genre needing specific planning and crafting. If you know that the test at your grade level typically asks students to write comparisons between two short texts, for example, build a unit of study around this type of writing. Your unit could be called, "Comparing Short Texts on Writing Tests." If you know that your students will likely be given a prompt that asks for persuasive writing, make sure that you have included a persuasive essay unit of study in your yearlong plan. In a unit of this nature, you'll want to address test-taking skills such as reading and comprehending, citing examples, and any other specific elements you know the scoring teams will look for.

UNIT-DESIGNED ASSESSMENTS

You should also design unit-based assessments. These will help you gather specific data about your students, which will aid you in designing future-focused instruction lessons and future writing conferences. Unit-based assessments also help you reflect on your own teaching, as you notice patterns in the data you collect. Finally, when made public within your classroom community, unit-based assessments help your writers edit and revise their writing pieces and also help them reflect on their own writing behaviors.

Checklists

A unit checklist can be easily created directly from the teaching points you have outlined for your unit. A checklist takes into account whether something is present in the writing piece or demonstrated by the writer himself. Because of the way you select your teaching points for each unit you design (some directly aligned to standards while others supplemental to the standards), the checklists will also naturally reflect your inclusion of above-standard writing skills. The checklist will hold your student writers accountable to the teaching points addressed in the unit. The message you give to your students by using checklists is "Here is a list of everything we learned in this unit. Every writer in this community should be incorporating these skills into their own writing work."

The most powerful unit checklists are created communally in the last few days of the unit (the commitment stage), during focused instruction or wrap ups. As you talk with your students about committing to the new learning going forward, put the journey you just completed in black and white on a chart. During a genre study this might mean listing the crucial elements of that genre. During a process unit, this might mean reviewing the behaviors of a successful writer. Resist the urge to create the checklist for your stu-

☑ list for Narratives
☐ A strong lead that hooks the reader into reading more
☐ Events in the order they happened
☐ Sensory details in all 5 senses
☐ Heart feelings (internal events)
☐ Transition words
☐ Words that tell why the event was important
☐ Showing sentences instead of telling sentences
☐ A strong closing that leaves the reader feeling like the story is finished

Collective creation of checklists boosts accountability to the skills.

Lesson Name: *Clean-Writing Checklist*

Unit Name: *Is My Writing Clean?*

Unit Type: *Strategy*   **Grade Level(s):** *K–2*

Focused Instruction: *"Okay, everyone, I know that we have this really nice new checklist in our room that helps to remind writers how to check to make sure their writing is clean." (Review conventions checklist.) "It's pretty, hanging there on the wall, but it isn't just for decoration. Today I am going to pretend that I'm a student, and I am going to show you how to use the checklist to make a piece of writing better. Watch." Model. Think aloud.*

Independent Practice: *Students use the checklist to edit for "clean writing."*

Wrap Up: *Pass out individual versions of the checklist and explain how students can use them by writing on them.*

dents. This is an excellent activity for the commitment stage of the unit. Let your students provide the information for the list by recalling the important elements of the unit. Fill in the gaps as needed.

Rubrics

Another excellent way to assess how your students respond to the units you teach is to design unit-based rubrics. Similar to checklists, your rubrics will include all of the teaching points from your focused period of study, including those that came from your immersion period. The major difference is that a rubric allows for

Narrative Rubric	1 ☺	2 ☺	3 ☺
Plan	none	sort of	yes
Details	none	1 or 2	more than 2 in order
Time Words	none	1 or 2	more than 2
Feelings	none	1	more than 1
Cool Moves	none	1	more than 1
5 Senses	none	tell	show

Rubrics outline a gradation of skill and can help to suggest specific areas for improvement.

gradation of the skills or teaching points you taught, while the checklist only assesses whether the skill is or is not present.

The assessment tool you design for your unit is your own professional decision to make. You may feel that a checklist is easier to use, or that a rubric is more flexible. You may decide that one type of tool is appropriate for certain units and another type of tool is more appropriate to the rest. You may feel that one of the tools is more suitable to the grade level you teach. Checklists might be a bit simpler to use, but rubrics also give children the chance to improve to the next stage of performance through clearly defined suggestions on how to improve a piece of writing or how to improve a writing process or strategy.

Easy-to-use charts invite students to utilize them authentically.

Make Them Visual!

You can drastically increase the chances that your wall charts and assessment tools will be used by your students if you include icons and other visual prompts. Attach an icon to each line item you write. These don't have to be fancy; a hand-drawn symbol or picture is all that is necessary (clip art works well, too). These visual prompts are of great help in the early grades, but will also trigger the memories of struggling readers, English learners, and special needs students in any grade.

Make Them Portable

Your checklists and rubrics, though tremendously helpful while displayed on the wall, can have more impact on your students and on your assessment if you also make portable, disposable copies with which your

Charts should be simple to use.

students can interact. You can make these after school, on your own time. After the class as a whole goes through the process of creating the checklist or rubric on a chart, sit at your computer and transcribe the data from the checklist or rubric onto one page. Print out copies and have them ready for your students during the focused instruction period the following day.

Your focused instruction lesson might sound something like this: "Yesterday we made our narrative checklist, and today I have a surprise for you. I took all the things you said should be in an excellent piece of narrative and put it all on a portable checklist that you can write on. As you look back over your narrative piece today, you can think about whether you have everything in it from the checklist. Make a check mark right on the paper when you find it. Then, you can use your list to go back and add the items you forgot. This way, you can be certain your writing piece is 'just right' before you add it to the class library!"

Portable versions of the assessment tools can be used in partner talks, group meetings, and conferences. They can also be sent home, so that parents understand clearly what is being taught during writing time and what is expected of their child in this area of his learning.

Assessment—Data to Be Shared

As you can see, I believe it is empowering for students to be in on the assessment process with you. Students must learn to reflect on their own behaviors and skills as writers. They benefit tremendously from looking within themselves and their writing products and from making critical decisions about the quality of their work. The assessment data you collect can and should be shared with the students themselves.

This self-reflection is crucial to the above-standard experience. All too often, our students carefully craft a piece of writing only to receive a score or letter grade on that piece of writing with no explanation about why. This is a tragic loss of opportunity for our students, once again placing them in a passive role instead of inviting them into a more active responsibility. All students deserve to know what they did right and how they can improve. We need to ensure that we are giving our students the message that writing, crafting, creating, and learning are infinite, inexhaustible processes during which action and feedback have a cyclical relationship.

Chapter 8

Integrating Standards to Make the Most of Your Time

"You really shouldn't judge someone from the outside until you go talk to them and find out what is in their insides. It takes time. Everyone has something good."
—Morgan, age 10

Have you ever heard anyone say, "This ain't no practice life!"? Though a rough way to put it, I think the message is quite poignant. These five words remind us that we're only here on this earth for a very short time, so we may as well try to make every second count.

This issue of time is one that has been on my mind a lot lately, as the mother of a toddler. My daughter is 14-months-old now, and when this book goes to market, she'll already be nearing her second birthday. She was only five pounds when she was born, so small that she slept snuggled into the hole of her Boppy pillow. She's about 20 pounds now, walking around saying things like "Shoes on," "Ni-night, Pop-Pop," and "Nice woof-woof!"

Where in the world does the time go?

Our relationships with the children in our lives, whether they are our own sons and daughters or our students, remind us how dear each stage really is. The various stages our children move through so quickly seem sadly brief at times. My daughter entertained us for about two weeks with what we called her chimpanzee walk. In her first stage of walking, when she was only starting to figure it out, she wobbled all over the house with her arms curled up over her shoulders for balance—like a little chimpanzee. She soon found her confidence, and her arms lowered to a more natural state. Just like that, this charming little stage was over, and we were left with only video reminders to prove that it really did exist.

Time has extraordinary powers in the lives of kids. Children change before our very eyes, growing more capable and more independent every day. Many tired adults can attest to the fact that idle time is a novel idea to kids. They work diligently to fill every single second of their waking hours with physical and mental activity.

For teachers, whose lives are centered around childhood development, the sheer force of time is a constant presence—a frequently unwelcome visitor in the classroom. Teachers feel as though they have an inadequate amount of time to accomplish all they wish to accomplish, especially when incessantly taxed by the demands of meeting what may feel like an inordinate number of requirements in all areas of study. I hear this question from teachers all over the country: "How am I supposed to fit all of this in?" There is a collective feeling that in order to meet every obligation, we would have to extend the school week to seven days and the school day to ten hours (at least!).

Time is precious, indeed, but we can make the most of what we have by cleverly combining many teaching points under the same umbrella. We have already discussed how interrelated the reading and writing processes are. Though this book primarily addresses writing, I've suggested that reading and writing necessarily complement one another because the two skills are interdependent. By now you've seen just how rich these units can be, often meeting several standards at once. In this section, we will discuss further the impact of combining writing instruction with the content areas.

In life, writing rarely stands on its own. A small majority of people may take to writing for writing's sake. We can expect that a few of our students may make creative writing a career, entertaining with stories or contributing to major publications. Some of our students may incorporate writing into their lives as a private means of expression or an outlet for emotion. Chances are, though, that for most of our students writing will be a necessary aspect of another chosen path in life.

This generation needs writing skills more than any other generation before it. New careers, new technologies, and new literacies exist now which demand successful communication through writing. It is our responsibility to give this generation what they need to be successful in this ever-changing, post-modern world.

To fit all of this in, and to do so in a way that feels full and compelling, we can welcome the content areas into our writing discussion. Writing doesn't have to stand alone in our curriculum, but it is usually a better fit to bring the content areas into writing than it is to try and squeeze writing into the content areas.

New Literacies

So much of our school writing curriculum is dependent upon traditional literacies. We are asked to incorporate such genres as narrative writing and expository writing. We are required to teach such processes as partner editing, and such strategies as powerful word choice. Much of our curriculum is governed by the conventions and rules of language. In many cases, the writing standards we are using were adopted a few (or more) years ago. In this time of astonishing technical prowess, a few years may well represent a lifetime.

The traditional literacy skills included in our standards have stood the test of time and are certainly crucial to the success of writing, but the world of literacy is changing every day. In fact, most states now have plunked technology standards right on top of the already mountainous piles of standards. Thought of separately, these two sets of standards (writing and technology) may seem overwhelmingly bulky, but when combined, they can complement one another.

In this discussion, we must consider the "new literacies"—those technological tools and ever-evolving skills all students need in this information age heavily influenced by the computer.

New Literacy Genres

- E-mail
- Web sites
- Personal Web pages
- Text messages
- Blogs
- Smartboards
- Magazines
- Video games
- Graphic novels
- Directions/operation manuals
- Synopsis texts (abstracts, summaries)
- Multigenre projects

Lesson Name: *Spell Check*

Unit Name: *Publishing With Technology*

Unit Type: *Strategy* **Grade Level(s):** *2–5*

Focused Instruction: *Explain what the spell-check feature does for writers. Demonstrate how to use the spell-check feature on your word processing program. Discuss the potential pitfalls of spell check and give examples of how it may not help, such as when a word is spelled correctly but not used correctly in a sentence.*

Independent Practice: *Students write on a word processing program, then spell check their passages.*

Wrap Up: *Students print out a passage after spell checking it, and check it themselves for spelling accuracy.*

Modern teachers must ask, "What can I do to incorporate the new literacies into my curriculum?" Another way we can push our writing curriculum above standard is to teach with the new literacies in mind.

NEW LITERACIES AS CHANNELS FOR DEEPER UNDERSTANDING

Literacy instruction should incorporate the new literacies.

Though it may be difficult because many of us hold traditional literacies near and dear to our hearts, inviting these new literacies into our classrooms will result in deeper understandings. Our students are already thinking in these ways. This generation is accustomed to information at its fingertips, quick bursts of detailed facts, and a feeling of being constantly available when friends and family request information.

Lesson Name: *Do I Hear a Tone?*

Unit Name: *Crafting Messages With Technology*

Unit Type: *Strategy*   **Grade Level(s):** *3–5*

Focused Instruction: *"Have any of you noticed how easy it is to miscommunicate when you are texting or e-mailing? This is an interesting way to communicate, because the listener (or reader) can't tell anything about your facial expressions, so you have to make sure they know your tone in your writing. You already do this in other kinds of writing, such as in narrative and poetry where you paint beautiful pictures with your words, but texts and e-mails are so much shorter, it's more challenging. How can we make people hear our tone in e-mails and texts?"* (Discuss creative use of punctuation, word choice, capital shouting, acronyms like "LOL," etc.)

Independent Practice: *If you have access to e-mail, students e-mail each other. If not, students can write quick e-mail or text-type notes to each other. Students try to emote in their notes.*

Wrap Up: *"What were some creative ways people made their tone heard?"*

As teachers of this generation, we can reflect upon these new literacies to further comprehend the types of skills our students need in order to be successful in the world today. What are the key understandings our students will require in order to create these types of texts? What type of process skills will they need? What genres are relevant to them? What strategies will aid their use of these new literacies? What conventions are significant?

NEW LITERACIES AS TOOLS FOR WRITTEN COMMUNICATION

You can incorporate these new literacies into your writing curriculum by thinking of them as tools for written communication. Ultimately, we want our students to be able to communicate in strong ways through writing. The tools they use to become successful writers are abundant in our world today. Where writers once had a rather small collection of tools such as the almanac, an

New Literacy Skills

- Synthesizing information from e-mails to add to a topic or conversation
- Researching on the Internet
- Reading critically to determine authority of a source
- Reading critically to determine accuracy of a source
- Scanning various genres for relevant information
- Creating a new idea from several sources
- Writing "tone" into informal communication
- Expressing humor and sarcasm in writing
- Writing scripts for video communication
- Writing dialogue for video games, graphic novels, etc.
- Understanding purpose and audience for various genres
- Writing on the same topic in various genres
- Writing to instruct or direct the actions of another
- Writing summaries and abstracts

encyclopedia, a dictionary and thesaurus, today information is available in a whole host of forms.

Consider a scenario. One of your students is at home with three friends discussing plans for the upcoming winter break. One friend explains that her family will travel to Durango, Colorado. Your student asks her friend to explain where that is. While it is possible that a simple verbal answer may follow this question, it is more likely that the four children will go straight to the computer to complete this conversation. They will search "Durango, Colorado," and they

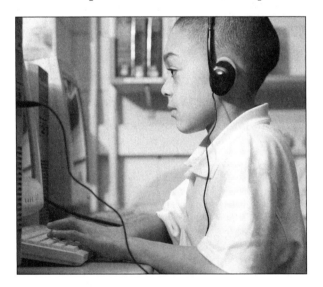

Our students are familiar with these new tools, so we should be, too.

will sort through a variety of Web sites, clicking on a few. They will learn (with the aid of colorful pictures and maps) not only where Durango is in the United States, but also where exactly it is on the world map. They will discover that their friend will need winter clothing for her trip because it could be as cold as 10 degrees in December. They will learn that she can snow ski while there, and that she can take a ride on the Silverton train. They will discover a blog written by Durango students their same age, and they will post the question, "I am coming to your city in December. What would you suggest that I see while I am there?" and they will wait for a real answer.

This is the informational world in which your students live, so your teaching should mimic it. Teaching students to research information, or to gather and collect data should include the authentic tools available to them. Is it necessary for your students to learn to flip the pages of an old encyclopedia? Certainly, if that is what your standards say, but if your standards simply refer to an "encyclopedia," then give some thought to using an electronic one. Should you teach about the thesaurus and dictionary? Sure, but don't forget these tools also exist on word processing programs, dictionary.com and thesaurus.com, and are much more likely the tools that are used when a child writes at home, or when an adult writes at work.

As you plan your units, make room for the many, many tools that students have available to them so that your instruction feels fresh and authentic to your students' way of life. Writing notes on index cards out of a World Book published in 1975 is sure to garner a few eye rolls from your sophisticated stu-

Lesson Name: *Researching Online*

Unit Name: *Nonfiction Writing*

Unit Type: *Genre*   **Grade Level(s):** *K–2*

Focused Instruction: *Even our youngest students can research online. During a genre unit on nonfiction writing, have your students research online for information about the subject of their report. Go to the computer lab and teach them to search for age-appropriate information in an electronic encyclopedia or on a safe Internet site you have preselected.*

Independent Practice: *Have each student print out an information sheet to take back and use in their reports. Students can learn to highlight information or cut out photographs for the report.*

Wrap Up: *Discuss why researching online is faster and more encompassing than in books.*

FROM THE PLAN BOOK

Ways to Incorporate New Literacies as "Tools" Into Your Units of Study

- In a genre unit on expository writing, teach your students to research online or on an encyclopedia software program.
- In a process unit on peer conferring, teach students to e-mail texts to each other and to use the editing tools on your word processing software.
- In a strategy unit on word choice, teach your students to use the thesaurus tool on your word processing software.
- In a conventions unit on end punctuation, teach your students what those green squiggly underlines mean (the ones that show up in text when there is a perceived mistake).
- Teach planning of writing using graphic-organizer software.
- Teach cutting and pasting.
- Teach students to do image searches and to include pictures and graphics in text.
- Help students take notes in online text.
- Model how to evaluate online sources of information and make judgments about their reliability (by looking for language like "official site" or by charting popular sites.)

dents these days. Children move quickly now, expect bundles of information packed into small containers, and multitask like never before. We have to be sure that we are giving them the tools to communicate in the modern world.

NEW LITERACIES AS END PRODUCTS IN YOUR UNITS OF STUDY

As previously discussed, it is important to identify the end product you wish your students to produce at the commitment stage of your unit. When planning for this, don't forget about the new literacies! As you teach your rich, above-standard units, consider requiring your students to demonstrate their new learning in a modern, interesting way. You can do this in a fancy or very simple way. A simple way to use technology to assist with commitment to new learning might be to have students write a sentence on a Smartboard. At the end of a comma unit, for example, each student could commit a sentence with proper comma usage to the board.

A more complex way to incorporate technology into an end product might be to require a multigenre project. If your state standards include at least a few traditional genres, for example, you might lead your students through an end-of-the-year unit where they create a Web page, blog, or magazine, a multigenre project where your students are required to write in various genres about one topic. For example, the final product of a multigenre unit of study could be a Web page about the environment that includes a poem, an informational article, and a short story.

Multigenre projects can also be quite involved. They can add dimension to your entire year if you decide that all of the units you plan over the year will eventually lead to this goal. Camille A. Allen's book *The Multigenre Research Paper: Voice, Passion and Discovery in Grades 4–6* (2001) shows the ultimate strength of combining writing instruction with research, oral communication, and even art to support the common goal of a multigenre research paper.

I know a wonderful second-grade teacher who is incredibly innovative with using technology in his classroom. His students write, revise, edit, and

---

Ways to Incorporate New Literacies as End Products in Your Units of Study

- Teacher creates a class blog. Students contribute posts or comments.
- Teacher creates a class Web page, including links to student writing.
- Students write summaries of an online article.
- Students cite online sources in an expository piece.
- Partners fill in a T-chart (with one side labeled "Probably True" and the other labeled "Probably False") with online sources on a particular topic.
- Students discuss the accuracy of a source or piece of information.
- Students highlight relevant information from an article, individually on a photocopied sheet or collectively on the Smartboard.
- Students create (and write) a new idea from several sources.
- Students write an e-mail that embodies a specific teaching point such as "appropriate tone."
- Students write a blog comment that demonstrates a specific teaching point such as humor or sarcasm.
- Students produce a video or record a response on video.
- Students write a "Web site blurb" (like a book blurb but about a Web site).
- Students write a story entirely in cell phone text language.
- Students write directions to a video game.
- Class publishes a magazine about one topic.

publish throughout the year, but they don't stop at pinning their pieces on the wall or adding them to the classroom library. When students have finished their pieces, they scan them into the computer and record their voices reading them. Parents can later visit the class Web site, click on their children's writing pieces, and hear stirring renditions of them read by the authors themselves. These students also write lyrics to songs and perform them on camera accompanied by various musicians, including their teacher and other students.

You don't have to get fancy to incorporate the new literacies into your end products. Give some thought to both the tools that exist and to the skills that your students need in today's world.

INFUSING NEW LITERACIES IN YOUR UNITS OF STUDY

Aside from the overt ways you can address the new literacies, you can also infuse them throughout your entire year. As you design your units, lift them a bit higher by incorporating various experiences that address the rather sophisticated critical thinking, synthesizing of information, comparing of data and developing of ideas that our students not only need but are also naturally drawn to these days. This type of teaching has begun to trickle into the teaching of math in schools with the recent focus on discrete mathematics, a direct result of the computer influence on human logic. The time is now for these skills to be addressed within our literacy teaching as well. Our students' futures depend on it, and if our standards are not reflecting this type of skill quite yet, then we should supplement our curriculum with these new literacies.

Writing and the Content Areas

Another way to heighten the effectiveness of your teaching is to combine standards under the umbrella of one unit of study. By combining your writing standards with others from the content areas, you will enrich your units of study and use your teaching time in the most effective way possible. Give some thought to the content areas when planning your above-standard units. Writing isn't solely about communicating anymore. It is about processing information, synthesizing data, expressing tone, and so much more. Content areas such as science and social studies can give you the perfect vehicle for teaching writing skills. Writing has become a critical part of learning within the content areas.

WRITING AND SOCIAL STUDIES

Writing is a necessary and perhaps somewhat obvious part of teaching in Social Studies, and though many teachers will advocate integrating writing into social studies lessons, I think it more effective to turn this idea on its head and invite social studies into the writing curriculum instead. Because writing is so fluid and subjective, and because the subject of social studies is more solid and objective, I believe that social studies standards provide excellent subject matter for writing units. Consider two scenarios:

Scenario #1: Tacking Writing Onto a Social Studies Unit

Mrs. Smith's students are engaged in a social studies unit on famous Americans. For 30 minutes each afternoon for two weeks, students read about famous Americans in their textbooks. Students in Mrs. Smith's class visit the library and check out books on famous Americans. They read and discuss the influences these Americans have had on our country and why they were so influential. At the end of the unit, Mrs. Smith sends the following homework assignment home: "Write a biography of a famous American. Include reasons why this person was influential to American history."

Scenario #2: Inviting Social Studies Into the Writing Curriculum

Mr. Jones's students are engaged in a four-week unit of study on biographies. During the first week, the students are immersed in biographies, carefully noting the important elements of this genre. By the end of the week, the students in this class have listed ten important things that should be included in a biography: a timeline, the date and place of birth, early influences on the person's life, the person's major achievements, personal and professional information about the person, and much more. During the second week of the study, Mr. Jones uses anchor texts about historical figures to discuss the important elements of biographies and to instruct his students on how to include those elements in their own biographies. Through these discussions, and through exposure to many well-written anchor biographies about historical figures, Mr. Jones's students learn about the crafting of a biography while also learning about various historical figures. In the third week, each of Mr. Jones's students has selected his own historical figure and has begun writing a biography, developing a close relationship with the person of interest. Students have gathered information from various sources and are synthesizing this information into carefully crafted biographies on which they are coached daily. In the fourth week, students finish up their biographies. All of Mr. Jones's biographical authors share their work with their colleagues. These works are then added to a bin of anchor texts entitled "Biographies of Famous Historical Figures" for further review.

Mr. Jones Is Top of the Class

In scenario #2, Mr. Jones spends more of his valuable teaching time (60 minutes per day versus 30 minutes per day in scenario #1), but the time he devotes to this unit is exponentially more inclusive of various teaching points. In other words, Mr. Jones's unit is much more effective because it is broader in scope and includes many more standards by combining writing standards with social studies standards. Mrs. Smith in scenario #1 only focuses her efforts on social studies standards, not directly teaching any writing skill at all. Simply requiring her students to write a biography as homework does not constitute the teaching of the critical elements of a biographical text, nor does it teach them how to craft one of their own. Mrs. Smith seems to be leaving those teaching points up to the parents of her students.

Mr. Jones immerses his students in biographical text, allowing them to actively engage in defining the genre. These students have their hands on many examples of the types of books they will be crafting, and they are given the time they need to be inquisitive about biographical texts and to explore them for the answers to their questions. Meanwhile, Mr. Jones's students are also exposed daily to historical figures. Through exploring texts, discussing them with each other and their teacher, seeing examples of how authors crafted various sections of a biography,

Infusing social studies into the writing hour is a powerful way to meet two sets of standards at once.

> ### Ways to Invite Social Studies Into the Writing Curriculum
>
> - Use a social studies topic in a genre study such as expository reports, biographies, historical fiction stories, persuasive essays, speeches, or letters.
> - Ground a writing process (such as note-taking) in a social studies topic (such as the Civil War).
> - In a strategy unit on writing in response to prompts, give prompts that include social studies topics.
> - In a unit of study that requires research, include lessons that address synthesizing information from various sources.
> - Include social studies content vocabulary in the teaching of glossary writing or indexing.
> - When teaching summarizing, use articles about social studies topics such as the Civil Rights movement, slavery, the Holocaust.
> - Tap into student's emotions when possible, grounding such writing work as editorials, letters, and persuasive text in human-rights subjects such as poverty, educational access, and societal change.

Mr. Jones's students are learning about the subjects of the books themselves. By the time the unit has ended, the class has a huge collection of books about famous Americans that are well written and full of information.

WRITING AND SCIENCE

Like social studies, science can offer many powerful opportunities for writing. Though it may not be as easy to invite science into the writing work, it is possible to do so in ways that will enable you to make the most of your time by thinking in terms of combining standards into one unit. Science, being much more systematic, requires a different kind of writing altogether, a style of writing that is both relevant and important to the new literacies.

The science writing you can plan during writing time is probably best thought of as supplemental to the hands-on lab-type experiments you plan for your science period. Many of those experiments take a long time and are quite fun. They also require that your students record what is planned, what they predict will happen, and how the experiment pans out. This recording often takes a long time as well, particularly when you are teaching science in the early grades.

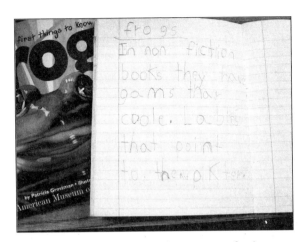

Students should be taught the nuances of science writing before they are required to do it.

I can remember teaching beautiful science lessons to my first graders at the end of a long day. The kids always loved the experiments, loved pretending they were little scientists digging up fossils or observing the world around them. I usually included some sort of recording sheet with these lessons, and when I reviewed these sheets after a hurried cleanup and send-off at the final bell, I was usually disappointed. They were messy, unreadable, and they didn't accurately represent the strong learning that occurred during the lesson. I finally figured out that it was because I hadn't yet taught my students the importance of science writing or the methods for science writing. Most of the time during these lessons, the focus was on the experiment itself, as it should have been, and not necessarily on the recording aspect.

This is where complementary, congruent planning of writing units can come in handy. After my unit of study on expository writing, in which my students explored such helpful tips as labels in illustrations, note jotting, and functional step-by-step writing, recording during science experiments was much less labor intensive, because my students knew what was expected and how to write this way.

WRITING AND SPECIALS SUCH AS MUSIC AND ART

A collective effort around a major subject such as writing can bring about astonishing results, turning ordinary students into extraordinary writers. A special kind of magic happens when an entire school wraps its arms around each and every student, setting high expectations and helping to keep students on the path toward greatness.

All members of a school staff have responsibilities, and I think it is essential that everyone support the important work done by all. But with subjects like reading or writing, skills that will predict a child's likelihood of dropping out early or her chances of going on to college, a collaborative

Ways to Support Science Writing With Your Writing Curriculum

- Call attention to descriptive definitions of science vocabulary.
- Use a science journal.
- Teach the art of brief note jotting (versus writing full sentences).
- Combine science with functional writing, including steps of an experiment.
- Model detailed illustrations with labels and captions.
- Design a genre study on expository writing, requiring students to write about a science topic from your science standards (e.g., a life-cycle book, a weather book, an animal book).

effort is an absolute duty. It doesn't even take much—just a little communication, commitment, and children's accountability to the skills they are being taught.

Teachers, let your specials teachers know what you are teaching in writing so that they can support the teaching you are doing. Many specials teachers are more than happy to scaffold your efforts. Tell your P.E. teacher when you start a unit on functional writing. Perhaps one of your students would like to turn his project into directions for a game. Let your music teacher know when you are writing poetry. Perhaps a special poem could be turned into a song. Explain to your art teacher when you are writing biographical essays. Maybe one of your students would like to research a favorite artist.

And by all means, get your librarians involved! Because so much of this teaching is dependent upon the glorious literature you will bring to life in your classroom, your librarian can be your most valuable ally. Librarians are on the literature front lines! They know what is new, what is good, and where to find the anchor books you will use as examples of your various teaching points. (They may even have budget money to order books!) Many librarians will even create your bin of anchor texts for you. Simply communicate that you are going to start a unit soon on striking verbs, for example, and ask if she can create a collection of literature that provides great examples of striking verbs.

When a school staff commits completely to above-standard teaching, above-standard results are inevitable. Strong leadership and communication can help everyone identify and commit to a common goal.

Conclusion:
Writing to New Heights

"What is the most important item in your whole house?" —*Mrs. Lera*
"Caring." —*Tommy, age 6*

During a unit of study on mimicking text structures, one of my students came to me for a conference. He was hard at work on his version of Todd Parr's *The Okay Book*. He had written a great many pages already, pages that tugged at the heartstrings, such as "It's okay to be me" and "It's okay to have brown skin," and "It's okay if you don't have a dad." Still, he came to this chat with a puzzled look on his face. He was really struggling with some aspect of his writing. I asked him what was troubling him and he said he thought he had an idea for his next page, but he wasn't sure it was appropriate. I told him to "hit me" and he said, "Can I write 'It's okay to have a unibrow?'" After my fits of laughter (and his, too—he didn't realize this was funny at all until he saw me almost fall off my chair and then he couldn't stop laughing either), I told him if he didn't write that, I'd write it in for him because it was too great to leave out. He started to leave the conference, and turned back. He asked, "Mrs. Lera, can I make my last page say, 'It's okay to love your teacher?'" I looked at this little creature of just seven through fresh tears and thought, "Child, you just reminded me why I teach." I said, "Of course."

Our children are too precious to this big world to allow standards and assessments to erase their personalities (or ours). Our elementary students are absolutely bursting with personality. Classrooms must support the unique people that fill them.

Teaching above standard means just this—it works to honor obligations while paying tribute to all that makes us human. By teaching above your standards, you not only meet your standards, but you do so in a way that still remains flexible enough to gently urge students to explore the world of writing and to begin to develop a sense of who they are in relation to that world of writing. Above-standard teaching enables to you to satisfy your obligations while still holding on to the joy and humor that makes your job a kick in the pants every day.

Hold on to that deep, unique sense of discovery—that is your right as a teacher! Pull up a chair alongside your students and look at the world through their eyes. You know that old saying, "Everything is better through the eyes of a child"? I think it's true! Welcome the silliness, glory in the kindness, cherish the creativity, relish the triumphs.

Know where you are going and hand the journey over to the travelers. Believe in them. My students never disappoint me. I have high expectations (usually much higher than my state standards) and my students usually exceed them. I think this is because the thought never enters anyone's mind that they won't make it to their destination. I just give my students the map and send them on their way. They wave to me as they pass through their destination and keep right on going.

But I learn, too. I learn all the time teaching this way. I learned one day that cats are immune to scorpion stings. Another day I learned that I didn't need to click the noisy left button on my laptop I've had for a year, because I have a touchpad mouse. (Duh, Mrs. Lera!) I was told when the Giants won and when an eclipse was expected. This is why I teach. I teach because I learn. I teach because I laugh. I teach because there is nothing standard about children.

The Complete 4 Standards Analysis Tool

Place your standards in the appropriate columns.

Process	Genre	Strategy	Conventions

Identifying Units of Study From Standards

Begin to cluster your standards into units of study.

Major	Unit Type	Minor	Standards Addressed

Above-Standard Unit Planner

Standards to Be Addressed by Unit

Complete 4 Category to Be Addressed by Unit: process   genre   strategy   conventions

Unit Major _____   Unit Minor _____

Unit Name _____

Standards-Based Unit Goals	

Teacher-Choice Unit Goals	

Student-Choice Unit Goals	

Unit Length _____

Unit End Product(s)

Above-Standard Lesson Template

Unit Name _____ Unit Length _____

Unit Type: Process   Genre   Strategy   Conventions

Unit Major _____ Unit Minor _____

DAY/STAGE	FOCUSED INSTRUCTION	INDEPENDENT PRACTICE	WRAP UP

The Above-Standard Year at a Glance

Schedule your units of study through your academic year.

August	
September	
October	
November	
December	
January	
February	
March	
April	
May	

My Writing Goal Sheet

Date Goal Set	Goal	I Did It!

My Writing Strengths

Name _____ Grade _____

What is your favorite genre to write? _____

Why? _____

What are your strongest writing habits?

_____

_____

_____

What are some strategies you use in your writing that make it strong?

_____

_____

_____

What writing conventions (writing rules) do you use strongly in your writing?

_____

_____

_____

Bibliography

Allen, C. (2001). *The multigenre research paper: Voice, passion and discovery in grades 4-6.* Portsmouth, NH: Heinemann

Allyn, P. (2007). *The complete 4 for literacy: How to teach reading and writing through daily lessons, monthly units, and yearlong calendars.* New York: Scholastic.

Allyn, P., et al. (2008). *The complete year in reading and writing, K-5 series.* New York: Scholastic.

Alston, L. (2008). *Why we teach.* New York: Scholastic.

Altrichter, H., Posch, P., & Somekh, B. (1993). *Teachers investigate their work: An introduction to the methods of action research.* New York: Routledge.

Anderson, C. (2000). *How's it going?: A practical guide to conferring with student writers.* Portsmouth, NH: Heinemann.

Arizona Department of Education. (2004). Arizona academic standards. Retrieved July 12, 2008, from http://www.ade.az.gov/standards/language-arts/writing/articulated.asp

Atwell, N. (2002). *Lessons that change writers.* Portsmouth, NH: Heinemann.

Atwell, N. (2007). *The reading zone: How to help kids become skilled, passionate, habitual, critical readers.* New York, NY: Scholastic.

Barth, R. (1990). *Improving schools from within.* San Francisco: Jossey-Bass.

California State Board of Education. English language arts standards, grades K-5. Retrieved July 9, 2008, from http://www.cde.ca.gov/BE/ST/SS/engmain.asp

Calkins, L. (1994). *The art of teaching writing.* Portsmouth, NH: Heinemann.

Calkins, L., with S. Harwayne. (1990). *Living between the lines.* Portsmouth, NH: Heinemann.

Collins, K., & Calkins, L. (2004). *Growing readers: Units of study in the primary classroom.* Portland, ME: Stenhouse.

Fletcher, R., & Portalupi, J. (1998). *Craft lessons: Teaching writing K-8.* Portland, ME: Stenhouse.

Fletcher, R., & Portalupi, J. (2001). *Nonfiction craft writing lessons: Teaching information writing K-8.* Portland, ME: Stenhouse.

Fountas, I., & Pinnell, G. S. (2006). *Teaching for comprehension and fluency: Thinking, talking, and writing about reading, K-8.* Portsmouth, NH: Heinemann.

Graves, D. (1983). *Writing: Teachers and children at work.* Portsmouth, NH: Heinemann.

Graves, D. (1994). *A fresh look at writing.* Portsmouth, NH: Heinemann.

Harris, D., and Carr, J. (1996). *How to use standards in the classroom.* Alexandria, VA: Association for Supervision and Curriculum Development.

Hart, L. (1983). *Human brain and human learning.* Village of Oak Creek, AZ: Books for Educators.

Harwayne, S. (1992). *Lasting impressions: Weaving literature into the writing workshop.* Portsmouth, NH: Heinemann.

Hindley, J. (1996). *In the company of children.* Portland, ME: Stenhouse.

Keene, E. O., & Zimmerman, S. (2007). *Mosaic of thought: The power of comprehension strategy instruction* (2nd ed.). Portsmouth, NH: Heinemann.

Kovalik, S., & Olsen, K. D. (2001). *Exceeding expectations: A user's guide to implementing brain research in the classroom.* Federal Way, WA: Susan Kovalik & Associates.

Leograndis, D. (2006). *Fluent writing: How to teach the art of pacing.* Portsmouth, NH: Heinemann.

Leograndis, D. (2008). *Launching the writing workshop: A step-by-step guide in photographs.* New York: Scholastic.

Miller, D. (2002). *Reading with meaning: Teaching comprehension in the primary grades.* Portland, ME: Stenhouse.

Moll, L. C. (1992). *Vygotsky and education: Instructional implications and applications of sociohistorical psychology.* Cambridge, UK: Cambridge University Press.

New York State Department of Education. Learning standards for English language arts. Retrieved July 13, 2008, from http://www.emsc.nysed.gov/ciai/ela/pub/elalearn.pdf

Pressley, M., Allington, R. L., Wharton-McDonald, R., Block, C. C., & Morrow, L. M. (2001). *Learning to read: Lessons from exemplary first-grade classrooms.* New York: Guilford.

Ray, K. W. (2001). *The writing workshop: Working through the hard parts (and they're all hard parts).* Urbana, IL: NCTE.

Ray, K. W. (2006). *Study driven: A framework for planning units of study in the writing workshop.* Portsmouth, NH: Heinemann.

Ray, K. W. (1999). *Wondrous words: Writers and writing in the elementary classroom.* Urbana, IL: NCTE.

Ray, K. W., & Cleaveland, L. B. (1999). *About the authors: Writing workshop with our youngest writers*. Portsmouth, NH: Heinemann.

Reeves, D. (2002). *The leader's guide to standards*. San Francisco: Jossey-Bass.

Sagor, R. (2003). *Motivating students and teachers in an era of standards*. Alexandria, VA: Association for Supervision and Curriculum Development.

Stengle, R. (2008). Mandela: His 8 lessons of leadership. In *Time, 172*(3), 42–48.

Texas Education Agency. (2001). Texas essential knowledge and skills. Retrieved July 2, 2008, from http://www.tea.state.tx.us/teks/

Children's Books

Bennett, K. (2005). *Not Norman: A goldfish story*. Cambridge, MA: Candlewick Press.

Brett, J. (1989). *The red mitten*. New York: G. P. Putnam.

Carrick, C. (1983). *Patrick's dinosaurs*. New York: Houghton Mifflin.

Chinn, K. (1995). *Sam and the lucky money*. New York: Lee and Low.

Creech, S. (1994). *Walk two moons*. New York: HarperCollins.

Creech, S. (2001). *Love that dog*. New York: HarperCollins.

Davies, N. (2001). *One tiny turtle*. Cambridge, MA: Candlewick Press.

Demi (1990). *The empty pot*. New York: Henry Holt.

Fleming, D. (2007). *Beetle bop*. Orlando, FL: Harcourt Books.

Fox, M. (1994). *Tough Boris*. Orlando, FL: Harcourt Brace.

Fox, M. (1995). *Wilfrid Gordon McDonald Partridge*. La Jolla, CA: Kane/Miller.

Fox, M. (1996). *Wombat divine*. New York: Harcourt Brace.

Frost, R. (1994). The road not taken. In G. Schmidt, (Ed.), *Poetry for young people: Robert Frost*. New York: Sterling.

Grossman, P. (1999). *Very first things to know about frogs*. New York: Workman.

Henkes, K. (2000). *Wemberly worried*. New York: Greenwillow Books.

Johnston, T. (2000). *Desert song*. San Francisco: Sierra Club Books for Children.

Katz, K. (2001). *Counting kisses*. New York: Simon & Schuster.

Komaiko, L. (1988). *Earl's too cool for me*. New York: Harper & Row.

Kraus, R. (1971). *Leo the late bloomer*. New York: HarperCollins Children's Books.

Martin, B., Jr., & Carle, E. (1996). *Brown bear, brown bear, what do you see?* New York: Henry Holt.

McMullen, K. and J. (2006) *I Stink!* New York: HarperTrophy.

Moffett, M. (2008). *Face to face with frogs*. Des Moines, IA: National Geographic Children's Books.

Munson, D. (2000). *Enemy pie*. San Francisco: Chronicle Books.

Nichol, B. (1993). *Beethoven lives upstairs*. New York: Orchard Books.

Numeroff, L. (1985). *If you give a mouse a cookie*. New York: Laura Geringer.

Parr, T. (1999). *The okay book*. New York: Little, Brown.

Parr, T. (2000). *Underwear do's and don'ts*. New York: Little, Brown.

Perry, S. (1995). *If*. Venice, CA: Getty Trust Publications With Children's Library Press.

Piven, H. (2007). *My dog is as smelly as dirty socks and other funny family portraits*. New York: Random House Press.

Raschka, C. (1993). *Yo! Yes?* New York: Orchard Books.

Ray, M. L. (2002). *All aboard*. New York: Little, Brown.

Reynolds, P. H. (2004). *Ish*. Cambridge, MA: Candlewick Press.

Rylant, C. (1996). *The whales*. New York: Scholastic/Blue Sky Press.

Rylant, C. (1985). *The relatives came*. New York: Simon and Schuster Books for Young Readers.

Rylant, C. (1995). *My mama had a dancing heart*. New York: Scholastic.

Rylant, C. (2000). *In November*. New York: Harcourt.

Sandburg, C. (1995). Fog. In F. S. Bolin (Ed.), *Poetry for young people: Carl Sandburg*. New York: Sterling.

Shannon, D. (2000). *No, David!* New York: Scholastic.

Shaw, C. (1947). *It looked like spilt milk*. New York: HarperCollins.

Silverstein, S. (1964). *The giving tree*. New York: HarperCollins.

St. Pierre, S. (2006). *What the sea saw*. Atlanta, GA: Peachtree.

Truss, L. (2007). *The girl's like spaghetti*. New York: G. P. Putnam's Sons.

Twain, M. (1948). *Huckleberry Finn*. New York: Grossett and Dunlap.

Vaughan, M. (2003). *I howl, I growl*. Flagstaff, AZ: Rising Moon.

Waddell, M. (1998). *The big, big sea*. Cambridge, MA: Candlewick Press.

Watt, M. (2007). *Chester*. Tonawanda, NY: Kids Can Press.

Wilkes, A. (1994). *Big book of dinosaurs: A first book for young children*. London: Dorling Kindersley.

Willems, M. (2003). *Don't let the pigeon drive the bus*. New York: Hyperion Children's Books.

Wise Brown, M. (1949). *The important book*. New York: HarperCollins.

Yolen, J. (1987). *Owl moon*. New York: Philomel.

Index